英語訳つき

おりがみ

Let's Enjoy Origami

in English and Japanese

山口 真
Yamaguchi Makoto

池田書店

伝えたい日本の心

さくら、つる、すもう…日本を代表するものが、
一枚の紙から生み出されます。
魔法のようですね。

さくらの器●Page100
CHERRY BLOSSOM CONTAINER

トントンすもう●Page30
SUMO GAME

ふうせん●Page28
BALLOON

つる●Page61
CRANE

INTRODUCING THE HEART OF JAPAN
Cherry blossoms, crane, sumo game ··· these all represent Japan.
Like magic, they emerge from a single sheet of paper.

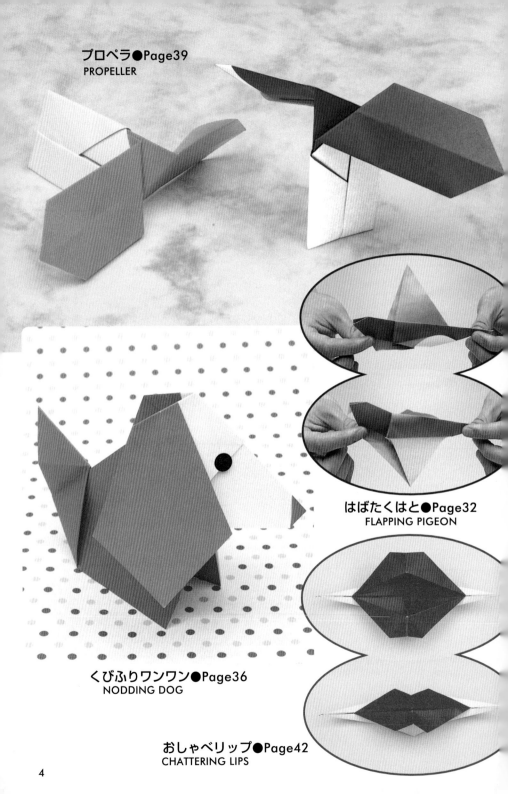

プロペラ●Page39
PROPELLER

はばたくはと●Page32
FLAPPING PIGEON

くびふりワンワン●Page36
NODDING DOG

おしゃべリップ●Page42
CHATTERING LIPS

動かして遊ぶおもちゃ
ACTION PLAY TOYS

紙の動きがユーモラスで、たの
しいものばかり。ことばよりも
早く心がつながりますね。

Origami action toys are lots
of fun to play with. Words
can't describe the delight
you'll instantly feel.

メリーゴーラウンド●Page45
MERRY GO ROUND

おしゃべりからす●Page34
TALKING CROW

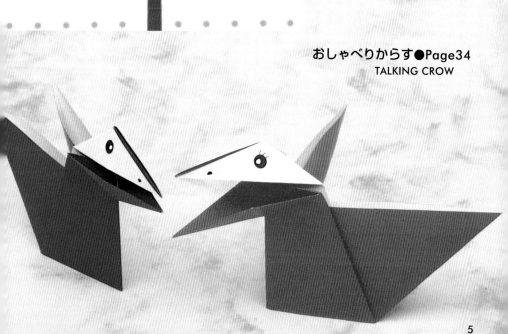

ほんの少しの工夫で、
どれもすてきな小物に早がわり。
大切な気持ちを伝えましょう。

心をこめてプレゼント

ワイシャツとネクタイ●Page120
DRESS SHIRT & NECKTIE

HEARTFELT PRESENTS

With just a little creativity, you can quickly transform a simple object
into something special. Show how much you care.

おしゃれなインテリア

FASHION INTERIOR
Surround yourself with original models and you'll swell with pride.

なべしき●Page110
POT HOLDER

フライドポテト●Page115
FRENCH FRIES

自分だけの、ちょっと自慢の
オリジナル作品に囲まれて
過ごしてみてはいかがですか。

ヨットの飾り方●Page53
YACHT／HOW TO DISPLAY

コースター（シングル）
●Page108
COASTER(SINGLE)

ハートのしおり●Page98
BOOKMARK HEART

ネコのしおり●Page96
BOOKMARK CAT

個性的
に
おもてなし

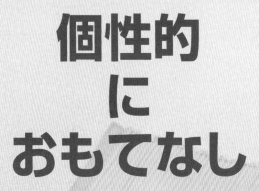

お客さまのイメージに合わせて、
テーブルセッティングを考えると、
わくわくしませんか？

コースター（ダブル）●Page108
COASTER(DOUBLE)

ハートのナプキンリング●Page106
HEART SHAPED NAPKIN RING

とりの入れ物●Page102
BIRD SHAPED CONTAINER

はしおき●Page105
CHOPSTICK REST

ナイフ＆フォークホルダー
●Page104
KNIFE & FORK HOLDER

PERSONAL TOUCH
Think about your guests
when setting the table.
They will appreciate the results.

ADORABLE CHRISTMAS

クリスマスツリー●Page140
STACKING CHRISTMAS TREE

かわいいクリスマス

小さなサンタやくつしたや星…
心のこもった手作りのクリスマスで聖夜を迎えましょう。

A tiny Santa Claus, sock and star … celebrate the holidays with models
handcrafted with care.

スノーマンのぼうし●Page128
SNOWMAN'S HAT

スノーマン●Page126
SNOWMAN

カード●Page133
CARD

スノーマンのミトン●Page129
SNOWMAN'S MITTEN

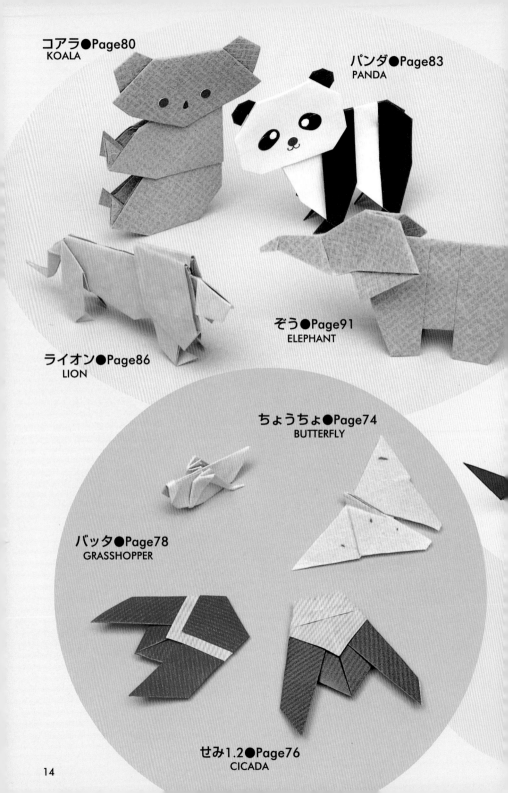

コアラ●Page80
KOALA

パンダ●Page83
PANDA

ぞう●Page91
ELEPHANT

ライオン●Page86
LION

ちょうちょ●Page74
BUTTERFLY

バッタ●Page78
GRASSHOPPER

せみ1.2●Page76
CICADA

生き物図鑑
LIVING DISPLAY

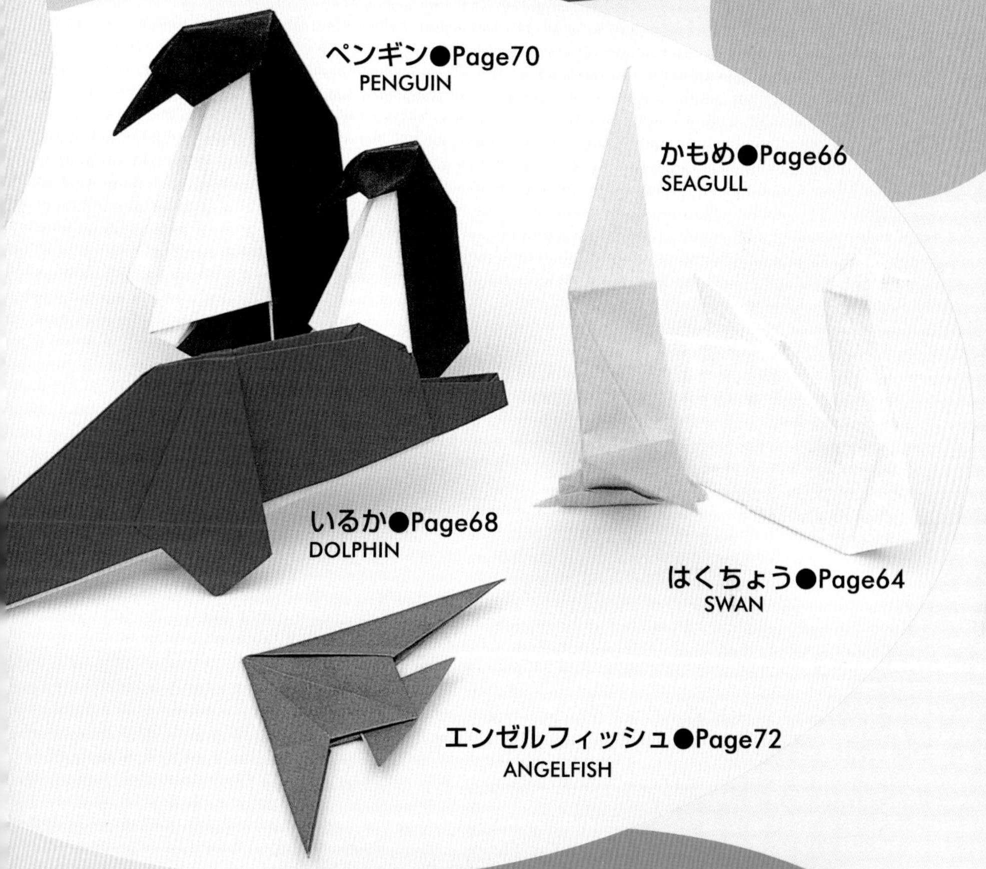

ペンギン●Page70
PENGUIN

かもめ●Page66
SEAGULL

いるか●Page68
DOLPHIN

はくちょう●Page64
SWAN

エンゼルフィッシュ●Page72
ANGELFISH

お気に入りの生き物を集めた
紙の昆虫館や動物園。
いつでもそばにいてくれる、
かわいい動物たちです。

Collect all your favorite living things
and make a paper insect museum or zoo.
These cute insects and animals will always be near you.

乗り物
TRANSPORTATION DISPLAY
図　鑑

ジェット機●Page56
JET AIRPLANE

コックピットつきヒコーキ●Page54
AIRPLANE WITH COCKPIT

スペースシャトル●Page58
SPACE SHUTTLE

ヨット●Page52
YACHT

ささぶね●Page50
BAMBOO BOAT

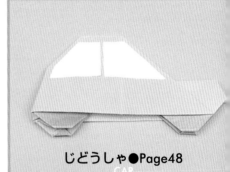

じどうしゃ●Page48
CAR

自分だけの
モーターショー開催中。
街へ海へ空へ、
空想の世界がどこまでも
広がります。

You can have your own motor show.
In the city, on the ocean, in the air …
expand your imagination.

はじめに

　「折り紙は日本のものですか?」とよく聞かれることがあります。これは結構難しい質問で、「紙を折る」ということ自体は日本特有のものではありません。なんとなく折っていれば何かの形になるもので、世界各地にそのような形で残され、手から手に伝わってきた作品はいくつかあるのです。しかし、「折り紙」を一つの文化、技法として育んできたのは日本であると私は思っています。

　私が30年程前、ヨーロッパを放浪していた頃には、折り紙はまだまだ一般的ではなく、「折り紙」という意味を説明するにも難しかったという記憶があります。しかし、今や「Origami」は世界に広がり、「Origami」という言葉が通じる国も多く、規模の大小は別にして世界二十数か国に折紙協会があり、その団体数も増えつつあります。また、イギリス、アメリカの折紙協会などは日本の折紙協会より歴史があるほどです。

　ある日本人がアメリカの知人に『折り鶴』を折ってあげたら、おかえしに「私が知っている鳥はこれ」と言って『羽ばたく鳥』を折ってもらった、などという話も聞きます。その日本人は鶴の折り方しか知らなかったそうです。こんな話を聞くたびに折り紙の広がりを感じ、またインターナショナルになっていく「Origami」の世界がとても楽しみになります。

　この本では、従来の「伝承折り紙」ばかりではなく、私の海外交流経験をもとに、人気があって、なおかつ気軽に折れる作品を集めてみました。折ったり、教えたりとコミュニケーションツールの一つとして利用していただければ幸いです。

山口　真

ORIGAMI BOOK INTRODUCTION

I am often asked, "Is origami a Japanese art?" This is a difficult question to answer. "Folding paper" is not limited to Japan only. When you fold paper, it transforms into various things, which can be done any place, anywhere in the world, passed on from person to person. However, I think "origami" have been fostered here as a part of the Japanese culture.

About 30 years ago when I was roaming in Europe, origami was relatively unknown. I remember how difficult it was to explain to people about origami. However, the word "origami" has spread throughout the world and today it is understood by many people. There are presently over 20 origami associations in the world and the numbers are increasing each year. Even, the British Origami Society and OrigamiUSA have more long history than NIPPON ORIGAMI ASSOCIATION.

I have heard the story of a Japanese person who, upon meeting an American, folded a " traditional crane" for their new acquaintance. The American, in turn, said, "this is what I can make" and folded a "flapping bird" for his new Japanese friend. The Japanese person only knew how to fold the traditional crane. When I heard this story, I realized how widespread origami had become. I am really looking forward to seeing the growth of origami as an international art form.

This book is not Japanese typical collection of origami models. I have discovered these models in my travels abroad. They are not only popular but also delightful to fold. Fold the models, then teach them to others. If you can learn this form of communication, you will be blessed with a satisfaction that no other art form can give.

YAMAGUCHI MAKOTO

Let's Enjoy Origami
in English and Japanese

もくじ   **CONTENTS**

カラー口絵・Color Frontispiece

遊ぶ・Play

Let's Enjoy Origami
in English and Japanese

もくじ　　　　　　　　　　CONTENTS

遊ぶ・Play

乗り物・Vehicle

生き物・Birds, Animals, Fish, Insects

19

生き物・Birds,Animals,Fish,Insects

使う・Use

もくじ　　　　　CONTENTS

Let's Enjoy Origami
in English and Japanese

もくじ　　　　　　　　　CONTENTS

使う・Use

飾る・Decorate

約束記号と基本の折り方

　折り紙の本を手にしたときに大切なことは、折り図を理解して作品を完成させるということです。そのためどうしてもおぼえてほしいことが、これから紹介する折り方の記号と基本の折り方です。むずかしいものではありませんから、折りはじめる前にぜひおぼえてください。

　美しい曲を奏でるには楽譜が必要なのと同様に、楽しい作品を折るのには折り図が必要です。記号をおぼえて楽しい作品を作ってください。

折り線の種類
TYPES OF CREASE LINES

折り線には谷折り線と山折り線の2種類があります。
There are two types of crease lines, mountain fold and valley fold.

谷折り線 -------------
Valley Fold

山折り線 ─ ∙ ─ ∙ ─ ∙ ─
Mountain Fold

手前に折る
Fold paper in front

後ろへ折る
Fold paper behind

谷折り
VALLEY FOLD

谷折り線を使って、矢印の方向に折ります。
To make valley fold, fold paper up in direction of arrow.

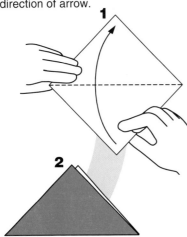

山折り
MOUNTAIN FOLD

山折り線を使って、矢印方向に折ります。
To make mountain fold, fold paper behind in direction of arrow.

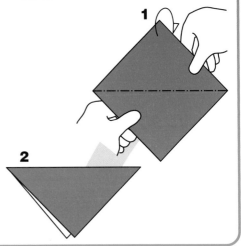

ORIGAMI SYMBOLS AND BASE FOLDS

When using an origami book, it is important to carefully follow the diagrams to complete your origami model. In order to do this, it is vital to understand the symbols used and know the origami base folds.Since there are no particularly difficult folds in this book, please learn the origami basics first.

Just as learning to play beautiful music requires an understanding of the written music, enjoying the art of folding paper requires an understanding of the diagrams. Learn the basic symbols and base folds first then you are on your way to making delightful origami.

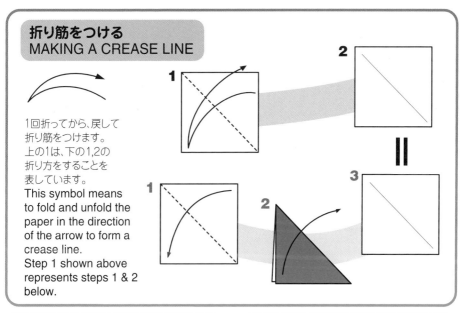

折り筋をつける
MAKING A CREASE LINE

1回折ってから、戻して折り筋をつけます。上の1は、下の1,2の折り方をすることを表しています。

This symbol means to fold and unfold the paper in the direction of the arrow to form a crease line.

Step 1 shown above represents steps 1 & 2 below.

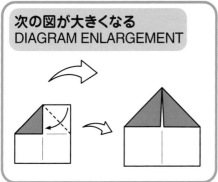

次の図が大きくなる
DIAGRAM ENLARGEMENT

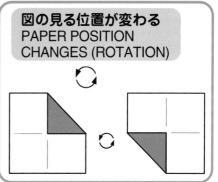

図の見る位置が変わる
PAPER POSITION CHANGES (ROTATION)

段折り
PLEAT FOLD

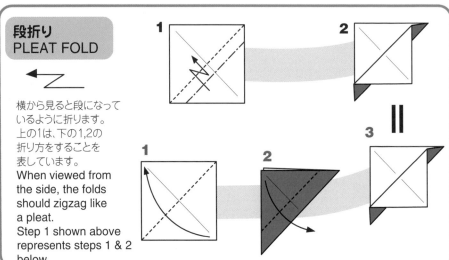

横から見ると段になって
いるように折ります。
上の1は、下の1,2の
折り方をすることを
表しています。
When viewed from
the side, the folds
should zigzag like
a pleat.
Step 1 shown above
represents steps 1 & 2
below.

裏返す
TURN PAPER OVER

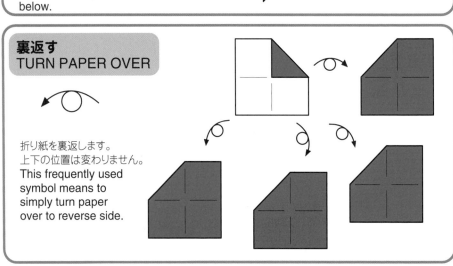

折り紙を裏返します。
上下の位置は変わりません。
This frequently used
symbol means to
simply turn paper
over to reverse side.

切る
CUT

切り込みを入れたりする
ときに使います。
This symbol is used
to indicate when cutting
is required.

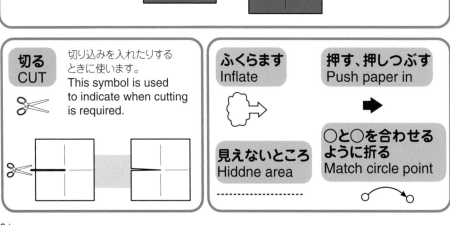

ふくらます
Inflate

押す、押しつぶす
Push paper in

見えないところ
Hiddne area

○と○を合わせる
ように折る
Match circle point

中わり折り
INSIDE-REVERSE FOLD

内側をわるようにしてカドを出して折ります。
Fold corner down in between layers
of paper until it protrudes from side.

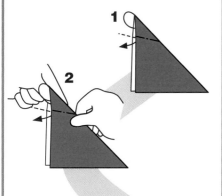

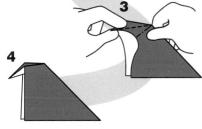

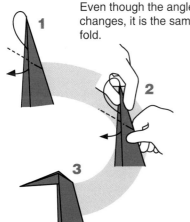

角度が変わっても
同じことです。
Even though the angle
changes, it is the same
fold.

かぶせ折り
OUTSIDE-REVERSE FOLD

内側をひらいてかぶせるように折ります。
Fold paper to the outside so that
the point covers the top.

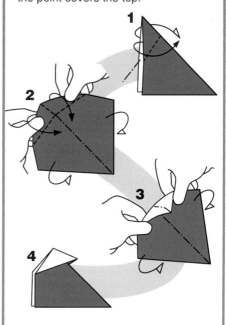

角度が変わっても
同じことです。
Even though the angle
changes, it is the same
fold.

この部分が山折りから
谷折りになります。
This portion of the point
reverses from mountain
fold to valley fold when
making outside-reverse
fold.

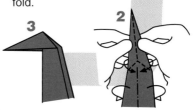

下の部分を出すように折る
RELEASE BOTTOM
FLAP WHEN MAKING FOLD

上の1は下の1、2を同時に
やります。
下のように折ってもかまい
ませんが、余計な筋がつき
ます。
In the diagrams shown
above, the bottom flap is
released to make the fold.
You can fold as shown
below, however, there will
be a crease in the flap
when it is unfolded.

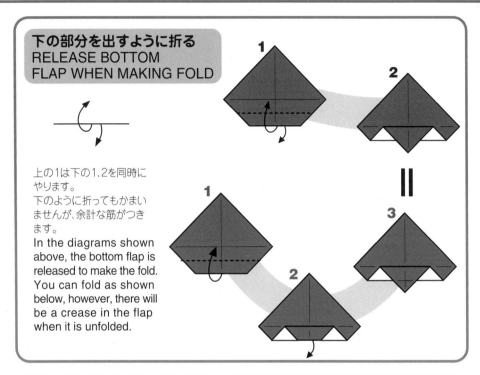

つまみ折り
RABBIT-EAR FOLD

内側をひろげてカドをつまむように折ります。
Lift top layer of paper, pinch corner
and fold flat into new position using
existing creases.

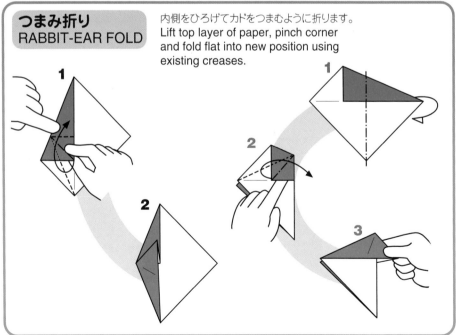

内側をひろげてつぶす
SQUASH FOLD

この折り方は角度が違ったり、一部分であったり
することもありますが、よく出てきます。
This type of fold occurs frequently in origami.
It is used on corners, top layers, etc.

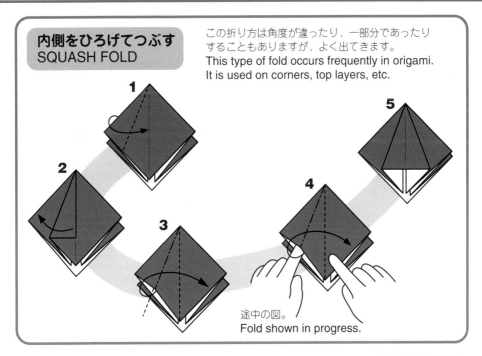

途中の図。
Fold shown in progress.

引き寄せ折り
SWIVEL FOLD

すきまに指を入れ、内側をひろげて矢印の方向に
折ってつぶします。
Insert your finger into the pocket to open up
fully then squash paper flat into position.

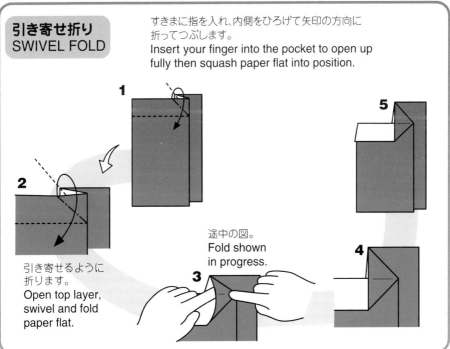

引き寄せるように
折ります。
Open top layer,
swivel and fold
paper flat.

途中の図。
Fold shown
in progress.

ふうせん
BALLOON

カラー口絵Page2-3

ふくらませたら、てのひらでぽんぽんとついて遊びます。大きさや色を変えて楽しみましょう。

You can play with this paper balloon by bouncing it in the palm of your hand.

紙・Paper Dimension
15cm×15cm・・・1

7

カドとカドを合わせて折る。
Fold corners of top layers to the top point.

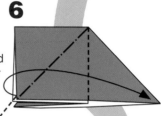

7

6

内側をひろげてつぶすように折る。
Open top layer and squash fold corner to the right.

6

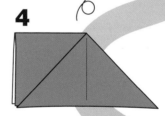

5

反対側に折る。
Fold flap on right all the way to the left.

5

4

1

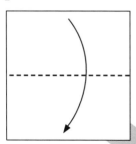

3

内側をひろげてつぶすように折る。
Open top layer and squash fold corner to the right.

3

1

半分に折る。
White side up, fold paper in half.

2

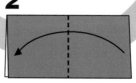

2

半分に折る。
Fold right side to the left side.

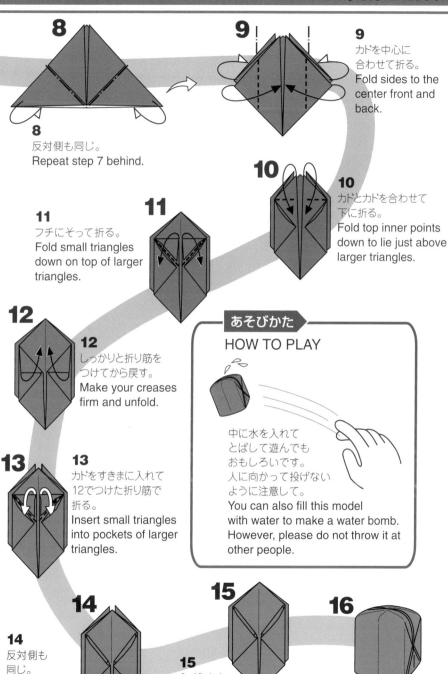

8

8
反対側も同じ。
Repeat step 7 behind.

9

9
カドを中心に
合わせて折る。
Fold sides to the
center front and
back.

10

10
カドとカドを合わせて
下に折る。
Fold top inner points
down to lie just above
larger triangles.

11

11
フチにそって折る。
Fold small triangles
down on top of larger
triangles.

12

12
しっかりと折り筋を
つけてから戻す。
Make your creases
firm and unfold.

13

13
カドをすきまに入れて
12でつけた折り筋で
折る。
Insert small triangles
into pockets of larger
triangles.

あそびかた

HOW TO PLAY

中に水を入れて
とばして遊んでも
おもしろいです。
人に向かって投げない
ように注意して。
You can also fill this model
with water to make a water bomb.
However, please do not throw it at
other people.

14

14
反対側も
同じ。
Repeat steps
10-13 behind.

15

15
ふくらます。
Inflate balloon
at bottom.

16

できあがり
Model complete

トントン
すもう
SUMO
GAME

カラー口絵Page3

日本の国技であるすもうをおりがみで折って遊びます。しっかり折って強いおすもうさんを作りましょう。

You can re-enact the Japanese national game of Sumo with these models. Make your folds firmly and you will have a strong Sumo wrestler.

紙・Paper Dimension
15cm×15cm···2

6
途中の図。
反対側も
同じ。
Step 5 folding
in progress.

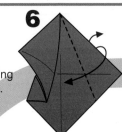

5
下のカドを出すように
フチを中心に
合わせて折る。
Fold upper folded edges
to the center while
releasing the back flaps.

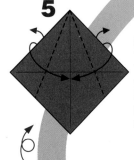

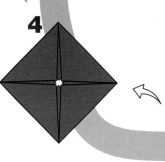

3
カドを中心に合わせて
折る。
Fold all four corners
to the center.

1
三角に
折り筋をつける。
White side up, fold in half
diagonally both ways and unfold.

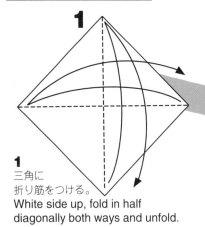

2
カドを中心に
合わせて折る。
Fold all four
corners to the
center.

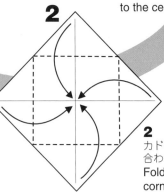

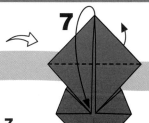

7

7
下のカドを
出すように
カドとカドを合わせて折る。
Fold top point down while
releasing point behind.

8

9

9
カドとカドを
結ぶ線で折る。
Fold bottom point up
between points at the
bottom as shown.

10

10
フチとフチを合わせて
折り筋をつける。
Fold left raw edge of
triangle down to the
bottom edge and unfold.

11

11
フチとフチを合わせて折る。
Fold right raw edge of
triangle down to the
bottom edge.

あそびかた

HOW TO PLAY

空き箱にまるをかいてどひょうを作ります。
Make a platform and draw a circle large
enough for two Sumo wrestlers.

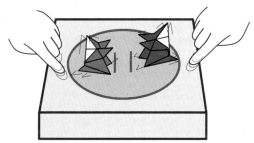

どひょうのはしを指でトントンたたいて
しょうぶします。先にまるから出たり、
たおれたりしたほうが負けです。
Tap on the platform with your fingers and
the Sumo wrestlers will jiggle about.
The first Sumo wrestler that moves outside
the ring or falls over loses.

14

できあがり
Model complete

13

13
カドをつまむように折る。
Pinch and pull the bottom
point to the right.

12

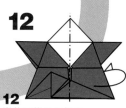

12
半分に後ろへ折る。
Mountain fold the model
in half to the back.

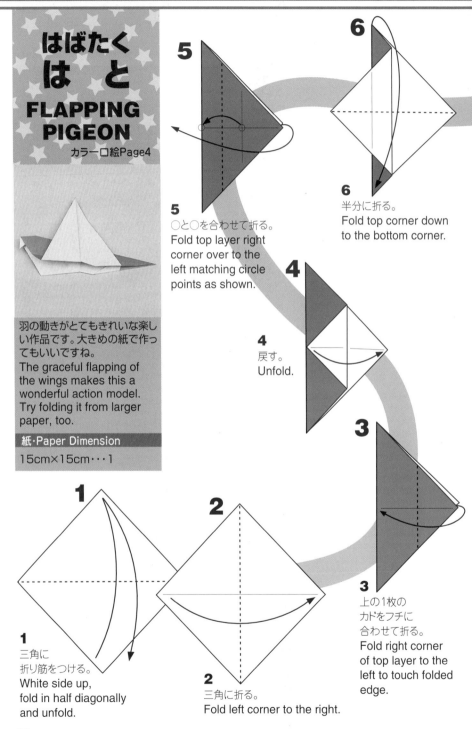

はばたく は と
FLAPPING PIGEON

カラー口絵Page4

羽の動きがとてもきれいな楽しい作品です。大きめの紙で作ってもいいですね。
The graceful flapping of the wings makes this a wonderful action model. Try folding it from larger paper, too.

紙·Paper Dimension

15cm×15cm・・・1

1
三角に
折り筋をつける。
White side up, fold in half diagonally and unfold.

2
三角に折る。
Fold left corner to the right.

3
上の1枚の
カドをフチに
合わせて折る。
Fold right corner of top layer to the left to touch folded edge.

4
戻す。
Unfold.

5
○と○を合わせて折る。
Fold top layer right corner over to the left matching circle points as shown.

6
半分に折る。
Fold top corner down to the bottom corner.

7

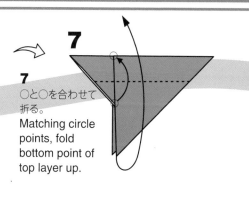

7

○と○を合わせて
折る。
Matching circle
points, fold
bottom point of
top layer up.

8

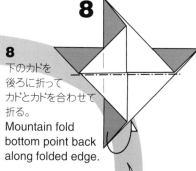

8

下のカドを
後ろに折って
カドとカドを合わせて
折る。
Mountain fold
bottom point back
along folded edge.

9

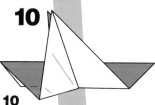

9

内側をひろげて
●を引き下げるように折る。
Swivel fold top layer of paper
down to fullest extent to
form point at top.

10

10

反対側も同じ。
Repeat step 9 behind.

あそびかた

HOW TO PLAY

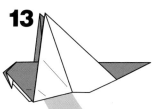

このカドのところを
つままないようにしましょう。
Do not hold the bird at
the circled point.

図のように持って、左右に引いたり
ゆるめたりすると、はばたいている
ように見えますね。
Using both hands, push and pull the
head and tail. The wings will flap like
a real bird.

13

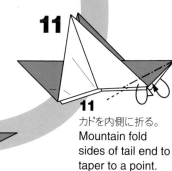

できあがり
Model complete

12

12

中わり折り。
Inside-reverse
fold the beak.

11

11

カドを内側に折る。
Mountain fold
sides of tail end to
taper to a point.

おしゃべり からす
TALKING CROW

カラー口絵Page5

お皿の上の豆をくちばしでつまんで取りあってもおもしろいでしょう。

This model can also pick up things in its beak. For fun, try your hand at picking up beans or other small objects from a plate.

紙・Paper Dimension

15cm×15cm・・・1

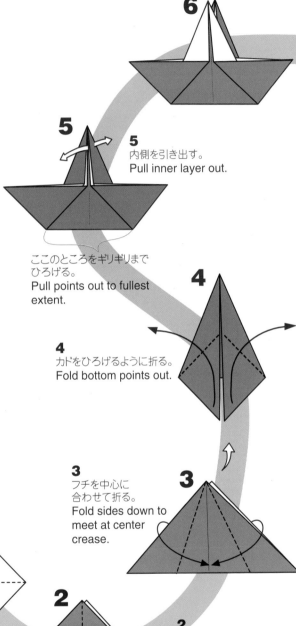

5
内側を引き出す。
Pull inner layer out.

ここのところをギリギリまでひろげる。
Pull points out to fullest extent.

4
カドをひろげるように折る。
Fold bottom points out.

3
フチを中心に合わせて折る。
Fold sides down to meet at center crease.

1
三角に折る。
White side up, fold in half diagonally.

2
三角に折り筋をつける。
Fold right point to the left point and unfold.

7

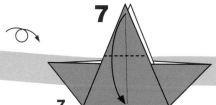

7
裏返して上の1枚の
カドをフチに合わせて折る。
Fold top point down to
touch bottom center line.

8

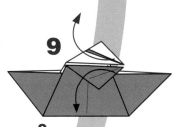

8
フチとフチを合わせて折る。
Fold upper and lower
folded edges to the right to
meet at center line.

あそびかた

HOW TO PLAY

羽を持ってひらいたり
とじたりすると、
くちばしをパクパク
させておしゃべりします。
Holding each wing, bring
them together and apart.
The mouth of the crow
will open and close like
it's talking.

9

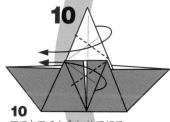

9
戻す。
Unfold both flaps.

10

10
フチとフチを合わせて折る。
Fold upper and lower
folded edges to the left
to meet at center line.

13

13
目と鼻をかく。
Draw in eyes
and nostrils.

できあがり
Model complete

12

12
カドをつまむように
折る。
Swivel fold upper and
lower points to the right
to form crow's beak.

11

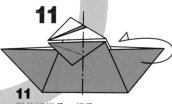

11
半分に後ろへ折る。
Mountain fold back the
right side on center crease.

くびふり ワンワン

NODDING DOG

カラー口絵Page4

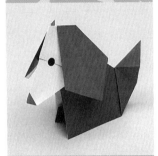

首をふってかわいい動きをします。スヌーピーに似たかわいいワンちゃんです。

This dog's head will wiggle on its body. Like Snoopy, it is very cute.

紙・Paper Dimension

15cm×15cm・・・2

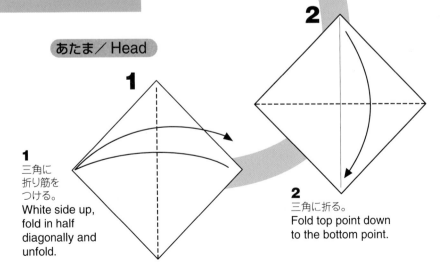

5

内側をひろげてつぶすように折る。
Open each side and squash fold evenly.

4

カドとカドを合わせて折る。
Fold both points down to the bottom point.

3

上の1枚だけカドを中心に合わせて折る。
Fold bottom point of top layer up to the center folded edge.

あたま／Head

1

三角に折り筋をつける。
White side up, fold in half diagonally and unfold.

2

三角に折る。
Fold top point down to the bottom point.

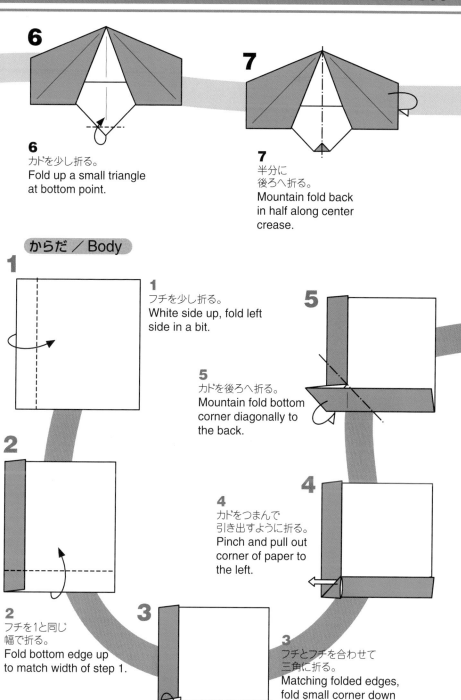

6

6
カドを少し折る。
Fold up a small triangle
at bottom point.

7

7
半分に
後ろへ折る。
Mountain fold back
in half along center
crease.

からだ ／ Body

1

1
フチを少し折る。
White side up, fold left
side in a bit.

5

5
カドを後ろへ折る。
Mountain fold bottom
corner diagonally to
the back.

2

2
フチを1と同じ
幅で折る。
Fold bottom edge up
to match width of step 1.

4
カドをつまんで
引き出すように折る。
Pinch and pull out
corner of paper to
the left.

3

3
フチとフチを合わせて
三角に折る。
Matching folded edges,
fold small corner down
to make a triangle.

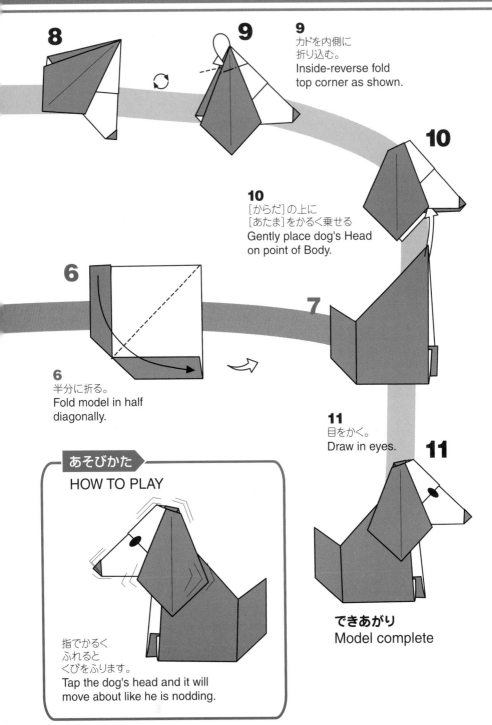

8

9

9
カドを内側に
折り込む。
Inside-reverse fold
top corner as shown.

10

10
［からだ］の上に
［あたま］をかるく乗せる
Gently place dog's Head
on point of Body.

6

7

6
半分に折る。
Fold model in half
diagonally.

11
目をかく。
Draw in eyes.

11

あそびかた
HOW TO PLAY

指でかるく
ふれると
くびをふります。
Tap the dog's head and it will
move about like he is nodding.

できあがり
Model complete

プロペラ
PROPELLER

カラー口絵Page4

小さい紙で折るときには薄い紙を使ってください。飛び方がきれいです。

Use thin paper if folding this model in a small size. It flies gracefully.

紙・Paper Dimension
15cm×15cm···1

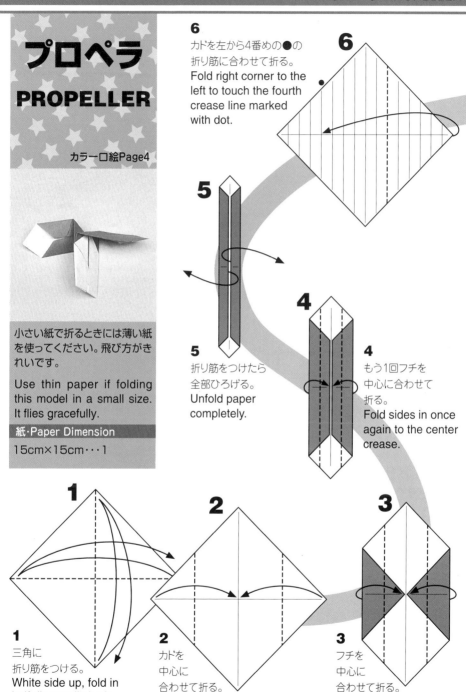

6
カドを左から4番めの●の折り筋に合わせて折る。
Fold right corner to the left to touch the fourth crease line marked with dot.

5
折り筋をつけたら全部ひろげる。
Unfold paper completely.

4
もう1回フチを中心に合わせて折る。
Fold sides in once again to the center crease.

1
三角に折り筋をつける。
White side up, fold in half diagonally both ways and unfold.

2
カドを中心に合わせて折る。
Fold corners in to the center crease.

3
フチを中心に合わせて折る。
Fold sides in to the center crease.

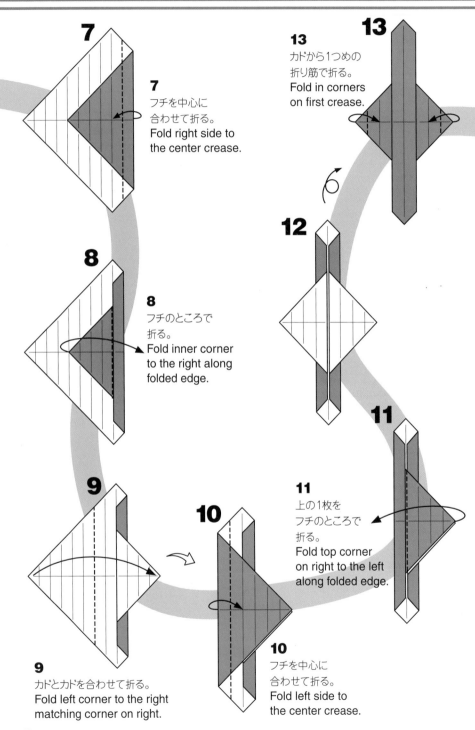

7

7
フチを中心に
合わせて折る。
Fold right side to
the center crease.

8

8
フチのところで
折る。
Fold inner corner
to the right along
folded edge.

9

9
カドとカドを合わせて折る。
Fold left corner to the right
matching corner on right.

10

10
フチを中心に
合わせて折る。
Fold left side to
the center crease.

11

11
上の1枚を
フチのところで
折る。
Fold top corner
on right to the left
along folded edge.

12

13

13
カドから1つめの
折り筋で折る。
Fold in corners
on first crease.

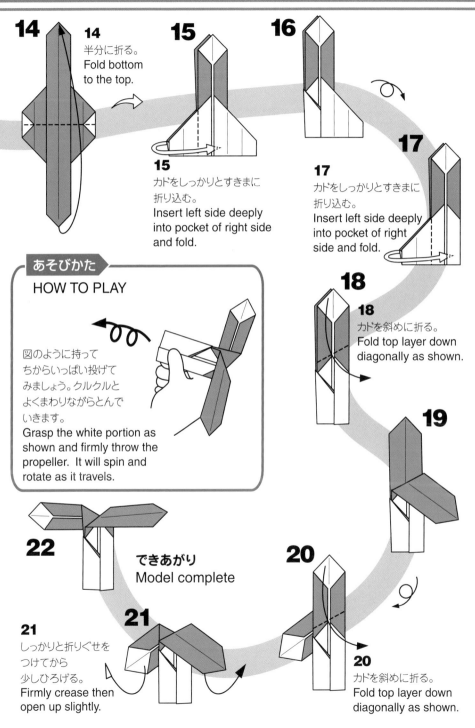

14

14
半分に折る。
Fold bottom
to the top.

15

15
カドをしっかりとすきまに
折り込む。
Insert left side deeply
into pocket of right side
and fold.

16

17

17
カドをしっかりとすきまに
折り込む。
Insert left side deeply
into pocket of right
side and fold.

あそびかた
HOW TO PLAY

図のように持って
ちからいっぱい投げて
みましょう。クルクルと
よくまわりながらとんで
いきます。
Grasp the white portion as
shown and firmly throw the
propeller. It will spin and
rotate as it travels.

18

18
カドを斜めに折る。
Fold top layer down
diagonally as shown.

19

20

20
カドを斜めに折る。
Fold top layer down
diagonally as shown.

21

21
しっかりと折りぐせを
つけてから
少しひろげる。
Firmly crease then
open up slightly.

22

できあがり
Model complete

41

おしゃべ リップ

CHATTERING LIPS

カラー口絵Page4

リアルな口びるがぱくぱく動く
楽しい作品です。表と裏で色の
違う紙を使うとよいでしょう。

This is a fun model that
moves just like real lips.
It is best folded from paper
with red on one side only to
achieve the two-tone affect.

紙・Paper Dimension

15cm×15cm・・・1

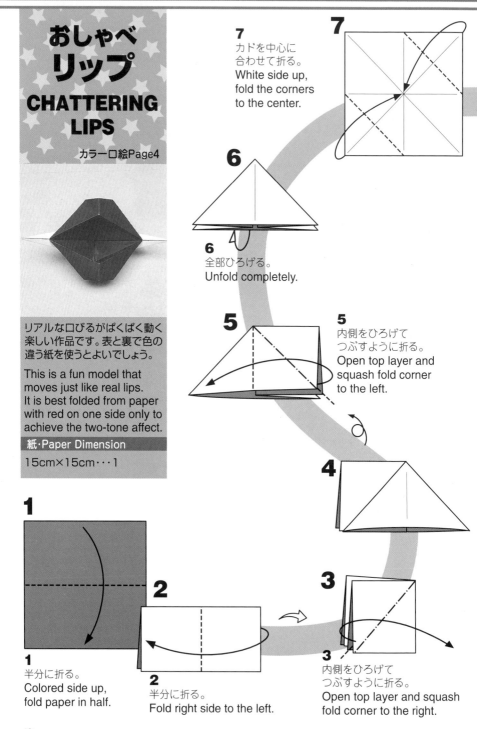

7
カドを中心に
合わせて折る。
White side up,
fold the corners
to the center.

6
全部ひろげる。
Unfold completely.

5
内側をひろげて
つぶすように折る。
Open top layer and
squash fold corner
to the left.

4

3
内側をひろげて
つぶすように折る。
Open top layer and squash
fold corner to the right.

1
半分に折る。
Colored side up,
fold paper in half.

2
半分に折る。
Fold right side to the left.

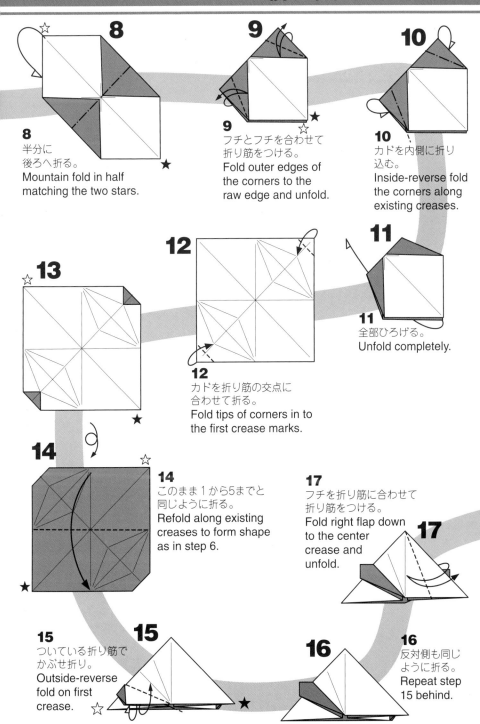

8
半分に
後ろへ折る。
Mountain fold in half
matching the two stars.

9
フチとフチを合わせて
折り筋をつける。
Fold outer edges of
the corners to the
raw edge and unfold.

10
カドを内側に折り
込む。
Inside-reverse fold
the corners along
existing creases.

11
全部ひろげる。
Unfold completely.

12
カドを折り筋の交点に
合わせて折る。
Fold tips of corners in to
the first crease marks.

14
このまま 1 から 5 までと
同じように折る。
Refold along existing
creases to form shape
as in step 6.

17
フチを折り筋に合わせて
折り筋をつける。
Fold right flap down
to the center
crease and
unfold.

15
ついている折り筋で
かぶせ折り。
Outside-reverse
fold on first
crease.

16
反対側も同じ
ように折る。
Repeat step
15 behind.

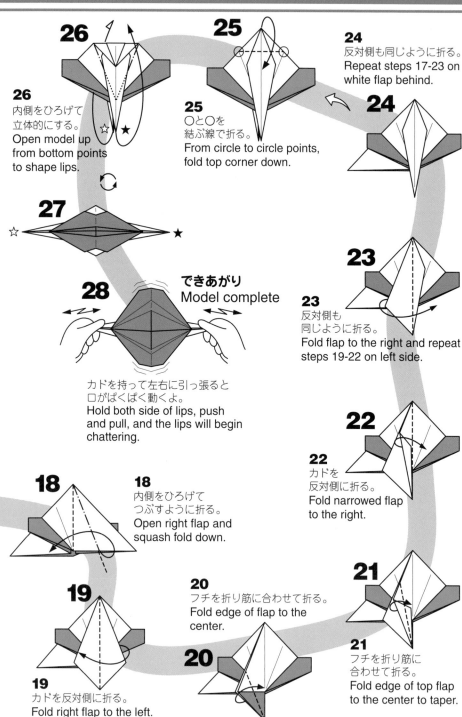

26
内側をひろげて
立体的にする。
Open model up
from bottom points
to shape lips.

25
○と○を
結ぶ線で折る。
From circle to circle points,
fold top corner down.

24
反対側も同じように折る。
Repeat steps 17-23 on
white flap behind.

27

28

できあがり
Model complete

カドを持って左右に引っ張ると
口がぱくぱく動くよ。
Hold both side of lips, push
and pull, and the lips will begin
chattering.

23
反対側も
同じように折る。
Fold flap to the right and repeat
steps 19-22 on left side.

22
カドを
反対側に折る。
Fold narrowed flap
to the right.

18
内側をひろげて
つぶすように折る。
Open right flap and
squash fold down.

20
フチを折り筋に合わせて折る。
Fold edge of flap to the
center.

21
フチを折り筋に
合わせて折る。
Fold edge of top flap
to the center to taper.

19
カドを反対側に折る。
Fold right flap to the left.

メリーゴーラウンド

MERRY GO ROUND

カラー口絵Page5

クルクルとよく回る、楽しいおもちゃになります。

This models spins well making it an enjoyable toy.

紙・Paper Dimension

15cm×15cm···2

紙の比率/Paper Proportions

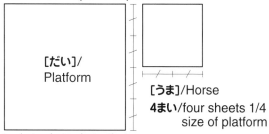

[だい]/
Platform

[うま]/Horse
4まい/four sheets 1/4
size of platform

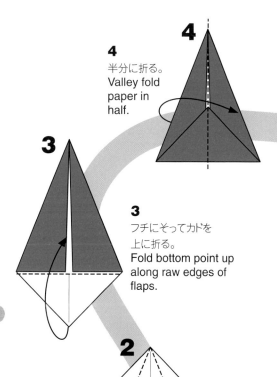

4

半分に折る。
Valley fold
paper in
half.

3

フチにそってカドを
上に折る。
Fold bottom point up
along raw edges of
flaps.

2

フチを中心に合わ
せて折る。
Fold top edges down
to meet at center crease.

うま／ Horse

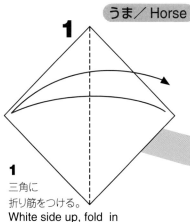

1

三角に
折り筋をつける。
White side up, fold in
half diagonally and unfold.

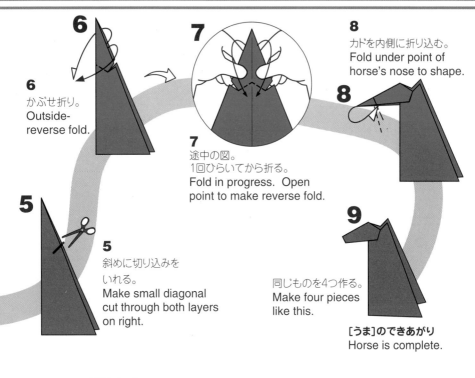

6
かぶせ折り。
Outside-reverse fold.

7
途中の図。
1回ひらいてから折る。
Fold in progress. Open point to make reverse fold.

8
カドを内側に折り込む。
Fold under point of horse's nose to shape.

5
斜めに切り込みをいれる。
Make small diagonal cut through both layers on right.

9
同じものを4つ作る。
Make four pieces like this.

[うま]のできあがり
Horse is complete.

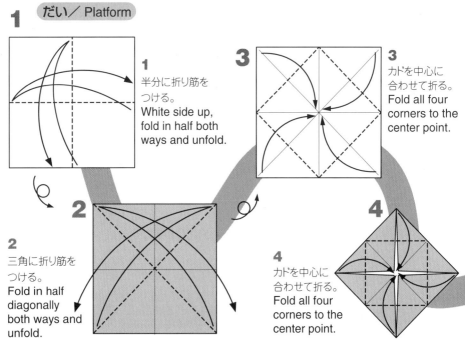

だい／ Platform

1
半分に折り筋をつける。
White side up, fold in half both ways and unfold.

2
三角に折り筋をつける。
Fold in half diagonally both ways and unfold.

3
カドを中心に合わせて折る。
Fold all four corners to the center point.

4
カドを中心に合わせて折る。
Fold all four corners to the center point.

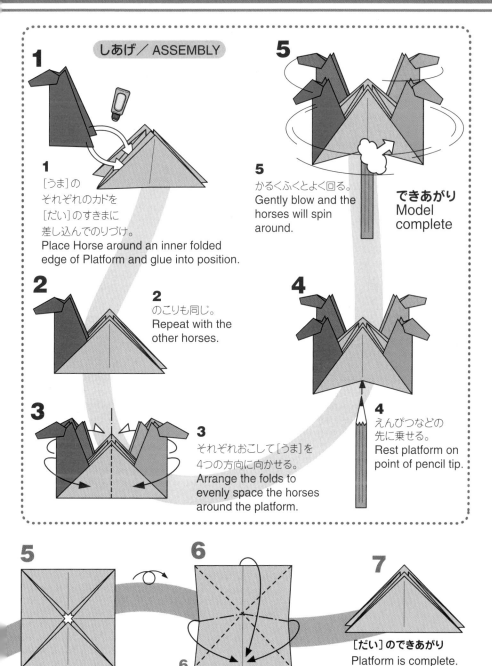

しあげ／ASSEMBLY

1

1
[うま]の
それぞれのカドを
[だい]のすきまに
差し込んでのりづけ。
Place Horse around an inner folded
edge of Platform and glue into position.

2

2
のこりも同じ。
Repeat with the
other horses.

3

3
それぞれおこして[うま]を
4つの方向に向かせる。
Arrange the folds to
evenly space the horses
around the platform.

5

5
かるくふくとよく回る。
Gently blow and the
horses will spin
around.

できあがり
Model
complete

4

4
えんぴつなどの
先に乗せる。
Rest platform on
point of pencil tip.

5

6

6
つけた折り筋を使ってたたむ。
Using existing creases,
collapse paper into shape.

7

[だい]のできあがり
Platform is complete.

47

じどうしゃ

CAR

カラー口絵Page16

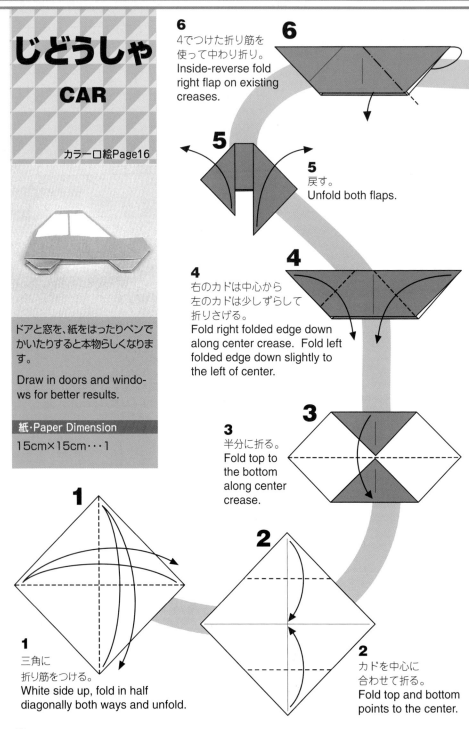

ドアと窓を、紙をはったりペンで
かいたりすると本物らしくなりま
す。

Draw in doors and windo-
ws for better results.

紙・Paper Dimension

15cm×15cm・・・1

6
4でつけた折り筋を
使って中わり折り。
Inside-reverse fold
right flap on existing
creases.

6

5

5
戻す。
Unfold both flaps.

4
右のカドは中心から
左のカドは少しずらして
折りさげる。
Fold right folded edge down
along center crease. Fold left
folded edge down slightly to
the left of center.

4

3
半分に折る。
Fold top to
the bottom
along center
crease.

3

1

2

1
三角に
折り筋をつける。
White side up, fold in half
diagonally both ways and unfold.

2
カドを中心に
合わせて折る。
Fold top and bottom
points to the center.

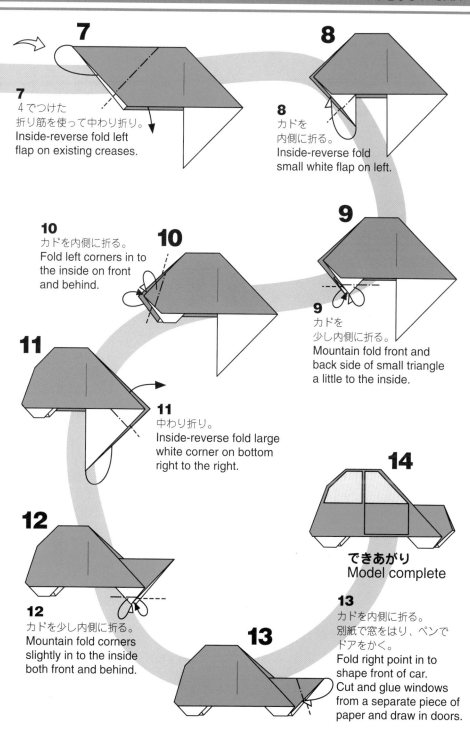

7

7
4でつけた
折り筋を使って中わり折り。
Inside-reverse fold left
flap on existing creases.

8

8
カドを
内側に折る。
Inside-reverse fold
small white flap on left.

10

10
カドを内側に折る。
Fold left corners in to
the inside on front
and behind.

9

9
カドを
少し内側に折る。
Mountain fold front and
back side of small triangle
a little to the inside.

11

11
中わり折り。
Inside-reverse fold large
white corner on bottom
right to the right.

12

12
カドを少し内側に折る。
Mountain fold corners
slightly in to the inside
both front and behind.

14

できあがり
Model complete

13

13
カドを内側に折る。
別紙で窓をはり、ペンで
ドアをかく。
Fold right point in to
shape front of car.
Cut and glue windows
from a separate piece of
paper and draw in doors.

ささぶね

BAMBOO BOAT

カラー口絵Page16

水に浮かべて遊ぶときには、折る前に外側にクレヨンを塗ると水をはじきます。

Before you place it in water, color the outside of the paper with wax crayon or other substance for durability.

紙·Paper Dimension

15cm×15cm···1

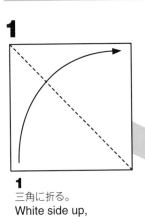

6
3でつけた
折り筋を使って
中わり折り。
Inside-reverse fold flap down on inner creases made in step 3.

5
2でつけた
折り筋を使って
中わり折り。
Inside-reverse fold flap up on creases made in step 2.

4
戻す。
Unfold flap.

3
フチとフチを合わせて折る。
Fold flap down to meet folded edge at bottom.

2
フチをカドに合わせて斜めに折る。
Fold up bottom folded edge at an angle.

1
三角に折る。
White side up, fold in half diagonally.

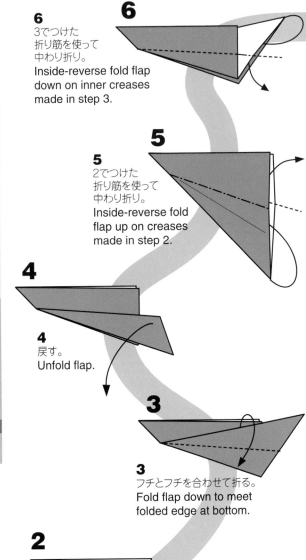
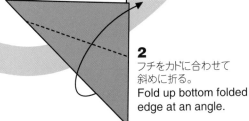

7

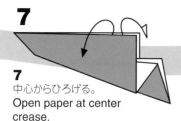

7
中心からひろげる。
Open paper at center
crease.

8

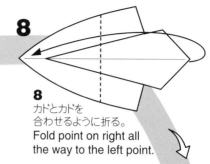

8
カドとカドを
合わせるように折る。
Fold point on right all
the way to the left point.

11

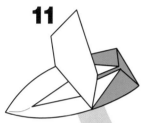

できあがり
Model complete

9

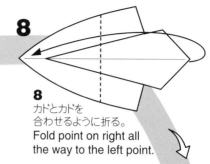

9
フチを中心に合わせて折る。
Fold upper and lower flaps
in to meet at center crease.

10

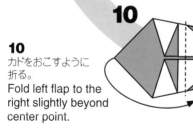

10
カドをおこすように
折る。
Fold left flap to the
right slightly beyond
center point.

あそびかた

HOW TO PLAY

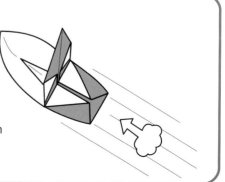

後ろからふくと、すいすい
進みます。つくえの上だけでなく
水の上などでも遊べます。
Blowing gently from the back, this
boat will glide not only across a
smooth desk top, but will also skim
the surface of water, etc.

ヨット
YACHT

カラー口絵Page16

とてもシンプルな作品です。カードなどにはって使ってもいいですね。

This is a simple model. It is suitable for decorating a card.

紙・Paper Dimension
大/Large: 5cm×5cm···1
小/Small: 4cm×4cm···1

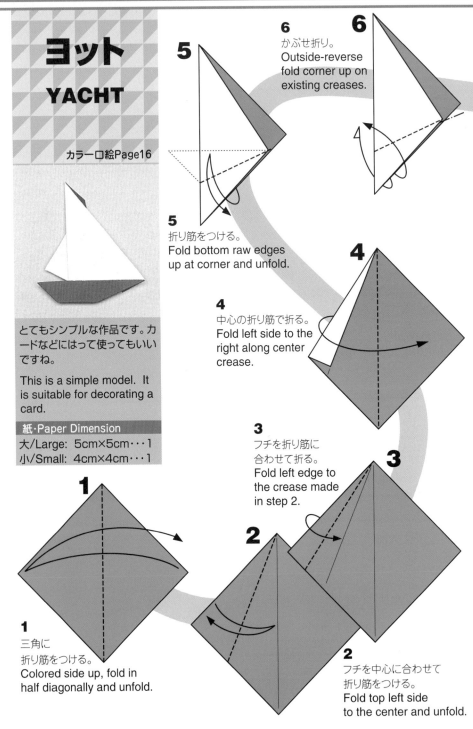

6

かぶせ折り。
Outside-reverse fold corner up on existing creases.

5

折り筋をつける。
Fold bottom raw edges up at corner and unfold.

4

中心の折り筋で折る。
Fold left side to the right along center crease.

3

フチを折り筋に合わせて折る。
Fold left edge to the crease made in step 2.

2

フチを中心に合わせて折り筋をつける。
Fold top left side to the center and unfold.

1

三角に折り筋をつける。
Colored side up, fold in half diagonally and unfold.

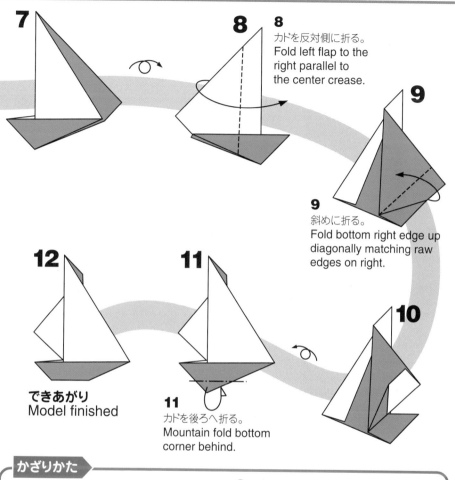

7

8

8
カドを反対側に折る。
Fold left flap to the right parallel to the center crease.

9

9
斜めに折る。
Fold bottom right edge up diagonally matching raw edges on right.

10

11

11
カドを後ろへ折る。
Mountain fold bottom corner behind.

12

できあがり
Model finished

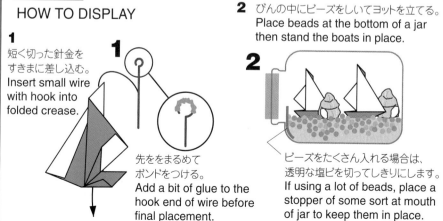

かざりかた

HOW TO DISPLAY

1

1
短く切った針金を
すきまに差し込む。
Insert small wire with hook into folded crease.

先ををまるめて
ボンドをつける。
Add a bit of glue to the hook end of wire before final placement.

2 びんの中にビーズをしいてヨットを立てる。
Place beads at the bottom of a jar then stand the boats in place.

2

ビーズをたくさん入れる場合は、
透明な塩ビを切ってしきりにします。
If using a lot of beads, place a stopper of some sort at mouth of jar to keep them in place.

53

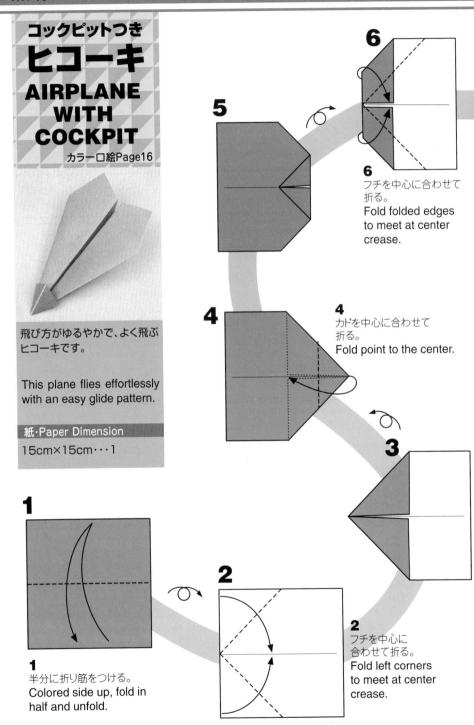

コックピットつき
ヒコーキ
AIRPLANE
WITH
COCKPIT
カラー口絵Page16

飛び方がゆるやかで、よく飛ぶ
ヒコーキです。

This plane flies effortlessly
with an easy glide pattern.

紙・Paper Dimension
15cm×15cm・・・1

6
6
フチを中心に合わせて
折る。
Fold folded edges
to meet at center
crease.

5

4
4
カドを中心に合わせて
折る。
Fold point to the center.

3

1
1
半分に折り筋をつける。
Colored side up, fold in
half and unfold.

2
2
フチを中心に
合わせて折る。
Fold left corners
to meet at center
crease.

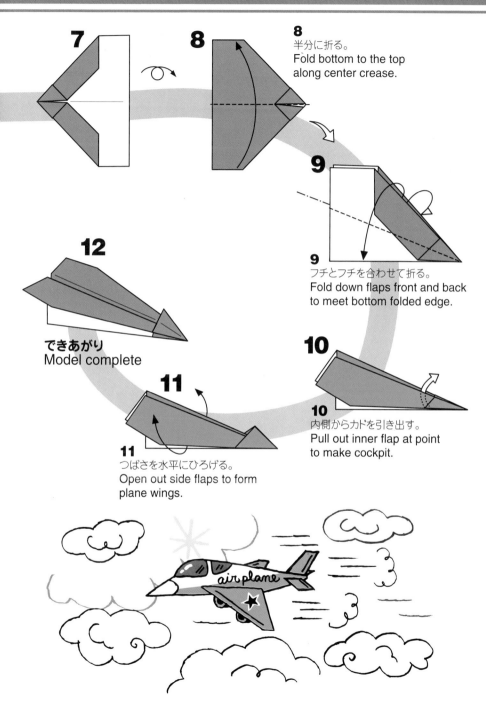

7

8

8
半分に折る。
Fold bottom to the top
along center crease.

9

9
フチとフチを合わせて折る。
Fold down flaps front and back
to meet bottom folded edge.

12

できあがり
Model complete

10

10
内側からカドを引き出す。
Pull out inner flap at point
to make cockpit.

11

11
つばさを水平にひろげる。
Open out side flaps to form
plane wings.

air plane

ジェット機

JET AIRPLANE

カラー口絵Page16

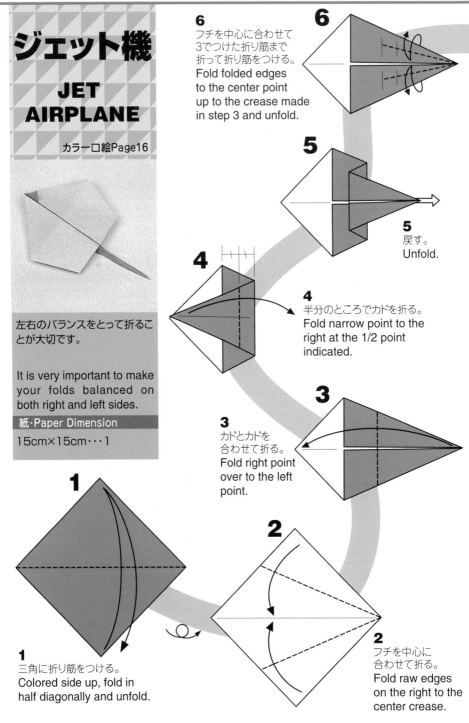

左右のバランスをとって折ることが大切です。

It is very important to make your folds balanced on both right and left sides.

紙・Paper Dimension

15cm×15cm・・・1

6
フチを中心に合わせて
3でつけた折り筋まで
折って折り筋をつける。
Fold folded edges
to the center point
up to the crease made
in step 3 and unfold.

6

5

5
戻す。
Unfold.

4

4
半分のところでカドを折る。
Fold narrow point to the
right at the 1/2 point
indicated.

3

3
カドとカドを
合わせて折る。
Fold right point
over to the left
point.

2

2
フチを中心に
合わせて折る。
Fold raw edges
on the right to the
center crease.

1

1
三角に折り筋をつける。
Colored side up, fold in
half diagonally and unfold.

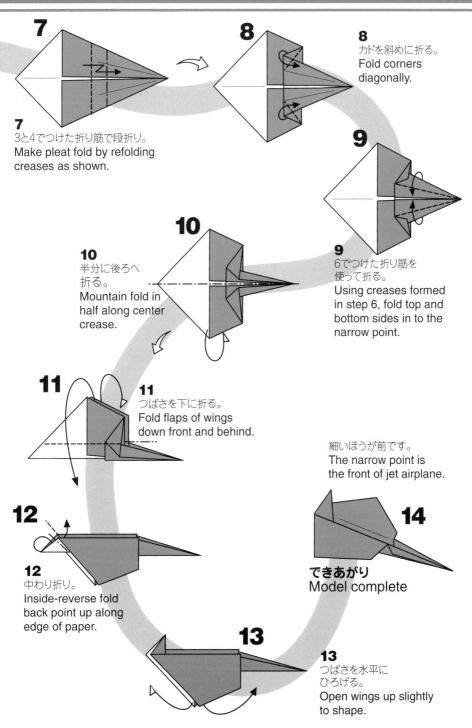

7

7
3と4でつけた折り筋で段折り。
Make pleat fold by refolding creases as shown.

8

8
カドを斜めに折る。
Fold corners diagonally.

9

9
6でつけた折り筋を使って折る。
Using creases formed in step 6, fold top and bottom sides in to the narrow point.

10

10
半分に後ろへ折る。
Mountain fold in half along center crease.

11

11
つばさを下に折る。
Fold flaps of wings down front and behind.

12

12
中わり折り。
Inside-reverse fold back point up along edge of paper.

13

13
つばさを水平にひろげる。
Open wings up slightly to shape.

細いほうが前です。
The narrow point is the front of jet airplane.

14

できあがり
Model complete

スペース シャトル
SPACE SHUTTLE

カラー口絵Page16

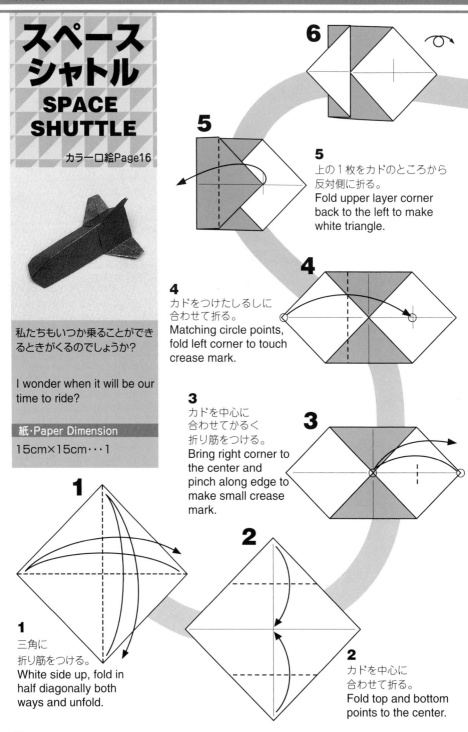

私たちもいつか乗ることができるときがくるのでしょうか?

I wonder when it will be our time to ride?

紙・Paper Dimension

15cm×15cm···1

1
三角に
折り筋をつける。
White side up, fold in
half diagonally both
ways and unfold.

2
カドを中心に
合わせて折る。
Fold top and bottom
points to the center.

3
カドを中心に
合わせてかるく
折り筋をつける。
Bring right corner to
the center and
pinch along edge to
make small crease
mark.

4
カドをつけたしるしに
合わせて折る。
Matching circle points,
fold left corner to touch
crease mark.

5
上の1枚をカドのところから
反対側に折る。
Fold upper layer corner
back to the left to make
white triangle.

6

58

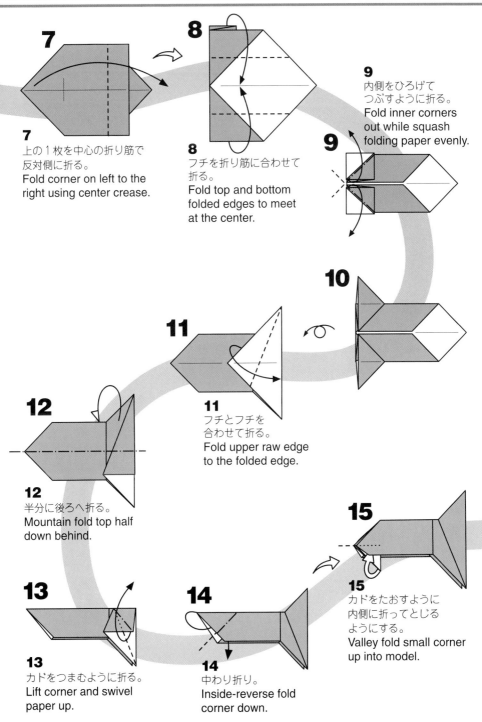

7

7
上の１枚を中心の折り筋で
反対側に折る。
Fold corner on left to the
right using center crease.

8

8
フチを折り筋に合わせて
折る。
Fold top and bottom
folded edges to meet
at the center.

9
内側をひろげて
つぶすように折る。
Fold inner corners
out while squash
folding paper evenly.

9

10

11

11
フチとフチを
合わせて折る。
Fold upper raw edge
to the folded edge.

12

12
半分に後ろへ折る。
Mountain fold top half
down behind.

13

13
カドをつまむように折る。
Lift corner and swivel
paper up.

14

14
中わり折り。
Inside-reverse fold
corner down.

15

15
カドをたおすように
内側に折ってとじる
ようにする。
Valley fold small corner
up into model.

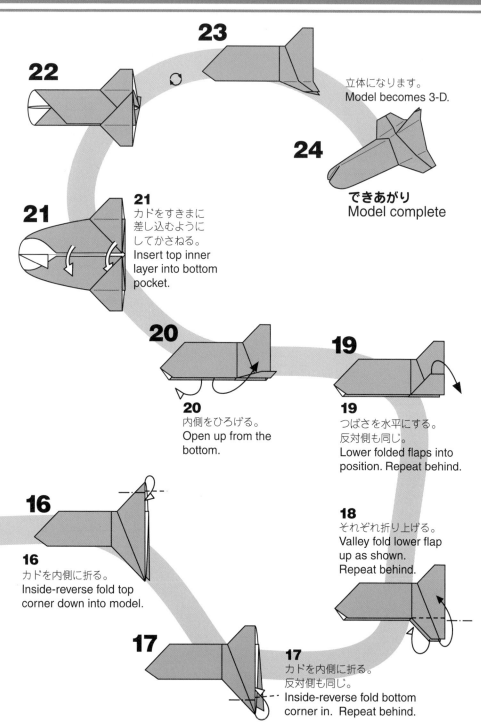

22

23

立体になります。
Model becomes 3-D.

24

21

21
カドをすきまに
差し込むように
してかさねる。
Insert top inner
layer into bottom
pocket.

できあがり
Model complete

20

20
内側をひろげる。
Open up from the
bottom.

19

19
つばさを水平にする。
反対側も同じ。
Lower folded flaps into
position. Repeat behind.

16

16
カドを内側に折る。
Inside-reverse fold top
corner down into model.

18
それぞれ折り上げる。
Valley fold lower flap
up as shown.
Repeat behind.

17

17
カドを内側に折る。
反対側も同じ。
Inside-reverse fold bottom
corner in. Repeat behind.

つる
CRANE

カラー口絵Page3

世界中で知られている作品。仕上げのときには背中をつぶさないように注意しましょう。
This is a worldwide well-known model. When opening up the finished model, avoid crushing the back.

紙・Paper Dimension
15cm×15cm‥‥1

6

6
内側をひろげて
つぶすように折る。
Open top layer and
squash fold left corner
to the bottom corner.

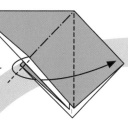

5

5
反対側に折る。
Fold right flap all
the way to the left.

4

3

3
内側をひろげて
つぶすように折る。
Open top layer and
squash fold left corner to
the bottom corner.

2

2
半分に折る。
Fold right corner
to the left.

1

1
三角に折る。
White side up, fold in
half diagonally.

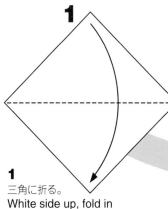

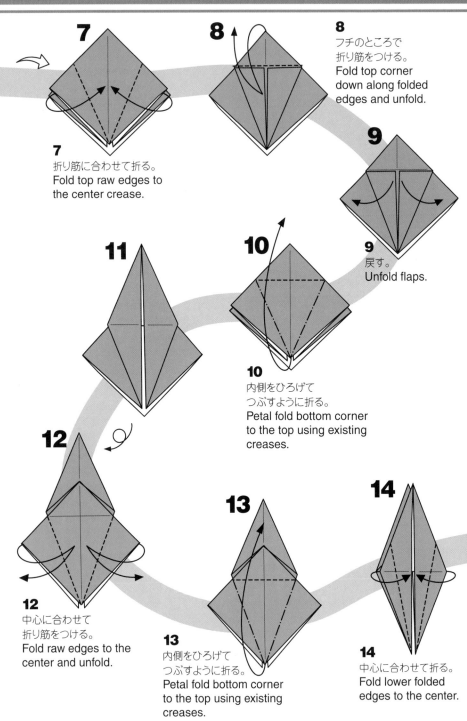

7

7
折り筋に合わせて折る。
Fold top raw edges to the center crease.

8

8
フチのところで折り筋をつける。
Fold top corner down along folded edges and unfold.

9

9
戻す。
Unfold flaps.

10

10
内側をひろげてつぶすように折る。
Petal fold bottom corner to the top using existing creases.

11

12

12
中心に合わせて折り筋をつける。
Fold raw edges to the center and unfold.

13

13
内側をひろげてつぶすように折る。
Petal fold bottom corner to the top using existing creases.

14

14
中心に合わせて折る。
Fold lower folded edges to the center.

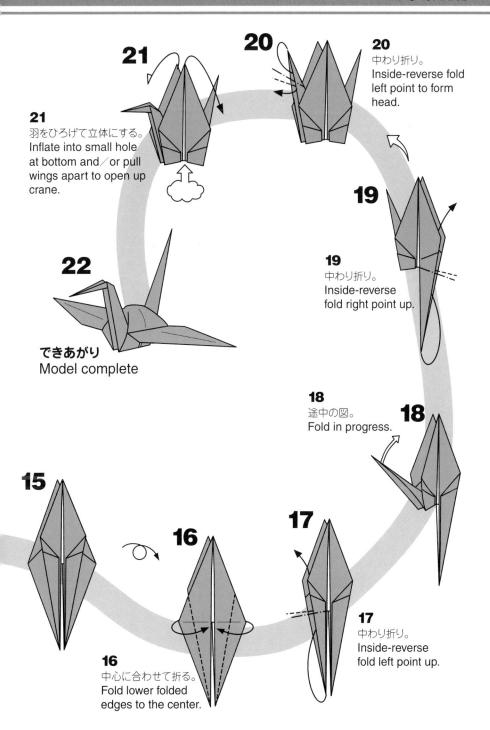

21

21
羽をひろげて立体にする。
Inflate into small hole
at bottom and／or pull
wings apart to open up
crane.

20

20
中わり折り。
Inside-reverse fold
left point to form
head.

22

できあがり
Model complete

19

19
中わり折り。
Inside-reverse
fold right point up.

18
途中の図。
Fold in progress.

18

15

16

17

16
中心に合わせて折る。
Fold lower folded
edges to the center.

17
中わり折り。
Inside-reverse
fold left point up.

はくちょう

SWAN

カラー口絵Page15

12の引き寄せ折りが少し難しいですが、図をよく見て折って下さい。

Step 12 is a little difficult to understand. However, if you follow the diagrams carefully, your swan will open up to final shape.

紙·Paper Dimension

15cm×15cm···1

6
内側のカドの
手前のところで
折る。
Fold left point to the right noting location of crease.

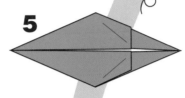

6

5

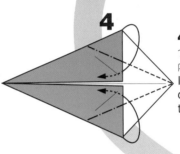

4

4
つけた折り筋を使って
内側へ折る。
Inside-reverse fold colored corners to the inside.

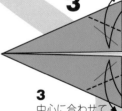

3

3
中心に合わせて
折り筋をつける。
Fold right sides to the center crease and unfold.

1

1
三角に
折り筋をつける。
White side up, fold in half diagonally both ways and unfold.

2

2
中心に合わせて折る。
Fold left sides to the center crease as shown.

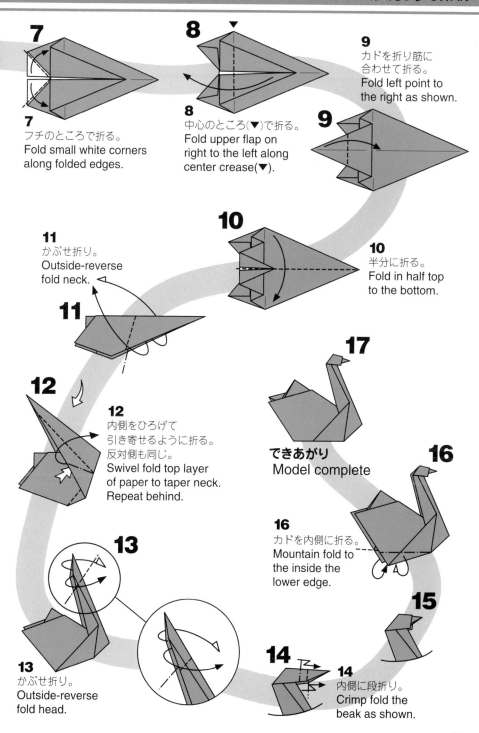

7
フチのところで折る。
Fold small white corners along folded edges.

8
中心のところ(▼)で折る。
Fold upper flap on right to the left along center crease(▼).

9
カドを折り筋に合わせて折る。
Fold left point to the right as shown.

11
かぶせ折り。
Outside-reverse fold neck.

10
半分に折る。
Fold in half top to the bottom.

17

12
内側をひろげて引き寄せるように折る。反対側も同じ。
Swivel fold top layer of paper to taper neck. Repeat behind.

できあがり
Model complete

16
カドを内側に折る。
Mountain fold to the inside the lower edge.

13
かぶせ折り。
Outside-reverse fold head.

14
内側に段折り。
Crimp fold the beak as shown.

15

65

かもめ
SEAGULL

カラー口絵Page15

海の上をすいすい飛ぶ鳥です。
インテリアとしても楽しめますね。

This bird flies over the ocean gracefully. As an indoor decoration, it is equally graceful.

紙・Paper Dimension

15cm×15cm…1

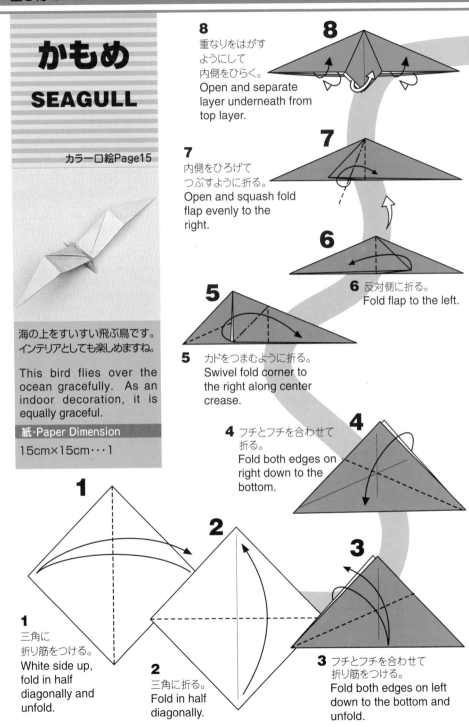

8
重なりをはがす
ようにして
内側をひらく。
Open and separate layer underneath from top layer.

7
内側をひろげて
つぶすように折る。
Open and squash fold flap evenly to the right.

6 反対側に折る。
Fold flap to the left.

5 カドをつまむように折る。
Swivel fold corner to the right along center crease.

4 フチとフチを合わせて折る。
Fold both edges on right down to the bottom.

1
三角に
折り筋をつける。
White side up, fold in half diagonally and unfold.

2
三角に折る。
Fold in half diagonally.

3 フチとフチを合わせて折り筋をつける。
Fold both edges on left down to the bottom and unfold.

66

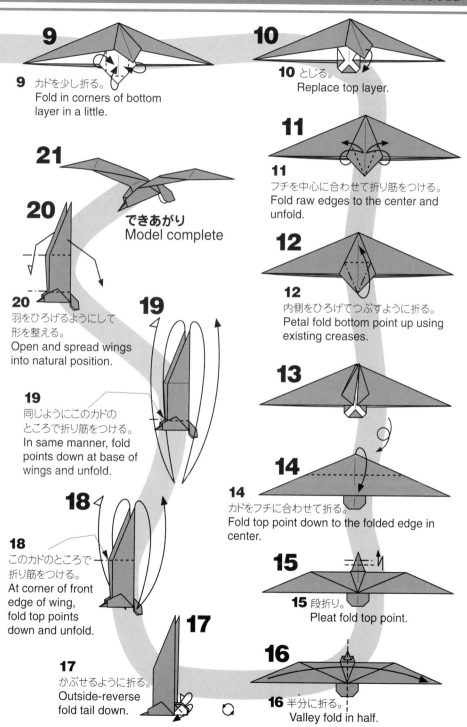

9
9 カドを少し折る。
Fold in corners of bottom
layer in a little.

10
10 とじる。
Replace top layer.

11
11 フチを中心に合わせて折り筋をつける。
Fold raw edges to the center and
unfold.

12
12 内側をひろげてつぶすように折る。
Petal fold bottom point up using
existing creases.

13

14
14 カドをフチに合わせて折る。
Fold top point down to the folded edge in
center.

15
15 段折り。
Pleat fold top point.

16
16 半分に折る。
Valley fold in half.

17
17 かぶせるように折る。
Outside-reverse
fold tail down.

18
18 このカドのところで
折り筋をつける。
At corner of front
edge of wing,
fold top points
down and unfold.

19
19 同じようにこのカドの
ところで折り筋をつける。
In same manner, fold
points down at base of
wings and unfold.

20
20 羽をひろげるようにして
形を整える。
Open and spread wings
into natural position.

21
できあがり
Model complete

いるか
DOLPHIN

カラー口絵Page15

いくつか作って並べると、いる
かたちが元気に遊んでいるよう
です。かわいいですね。

A number of these made
into mobiles in a window
make for a nice display.

紙・Paper Dimension

15cm×15cm…1

6

5
つけた折り筋を使って
カドを内側に折り込む。
Inside-reverse fold left
side using creases
made in step 3.

5

4
戻す。
Unfold.

4

3
反対側も同じように折る。
Fold left side of
paper towards
center in same
manner.

3

2
フチを中心より少し
手前に合わせて折る。
Fold right raw edges
towards center
crease leaving
a slight gap.

2

1

1
三角に折り筋を
つける。
White side up, fold in
half diagonally and
unfold.

ここを
少しあける。
Leave gap in
this area.

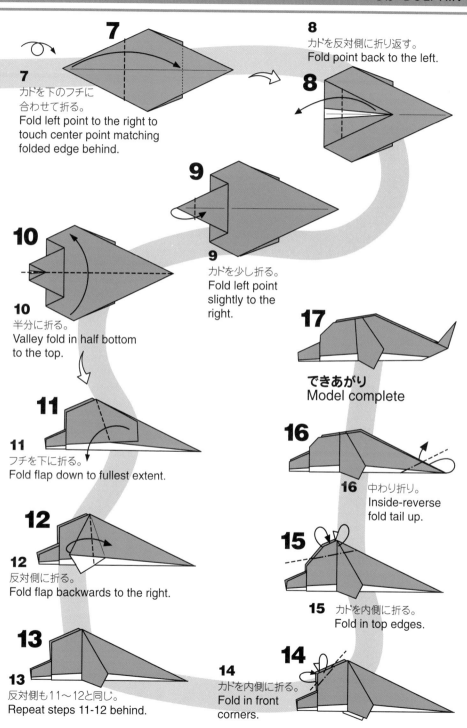

7

カドを下のフチに
合わせて折る。
Fold left point to the right to
touch center point matching
folded edge behind.

8

カドを反対側に折り返す。
Fold point back to the left.

9

カドを少し折る。
Fold left point
slightly to the
right.

10

半分に折る。
Valley fold in half bottom
to the top.

11

フチを下に折る。
Fold flap down to fullest extent.

12

反対側に折る。
Fold flap backwards to the right.

13

反対側も11～12と同じ。
Repeat steps 11-12 behind.

14

カドを内側に折る。
Fold in front
corners.

15

カドを内側に折る。
Fold in top edges.

16

中わり折り。
Inside-reverse
fold tail up.

17

できあがり
Model complete

69

ペンギン

PENGUIN

カラー口絵Page15

歩き方がかわいいペンギンです。この作品もそんな雰囲気をつかんでいますね。

This animal has a cute way of walking. That image is captured in this model of a penguin.

紙・Paper Dimension

15cm×15cm···1

6

折り筋の交わったところで折る。
Fold top point down at first intersection as shown.

6

5

5

フチを4でつけた折り筋に合わせて折り筋をつける。
Fold top edges down to the creases made in step 4 and unfold.

4

4

フチを1でつけた折り筋に合わせて折り筋をつける。
Fold top edges to the diagonal creases and unfold.

3

3

カドを中心に合わせて折る。
Fold bottom corner to the center.

1

2

1

半分に折り筋をつける。
White side up, fold in half both ways and unfold.

2

三角に折り筋をつける。
Fold in half right to the left diagonally and unfold.

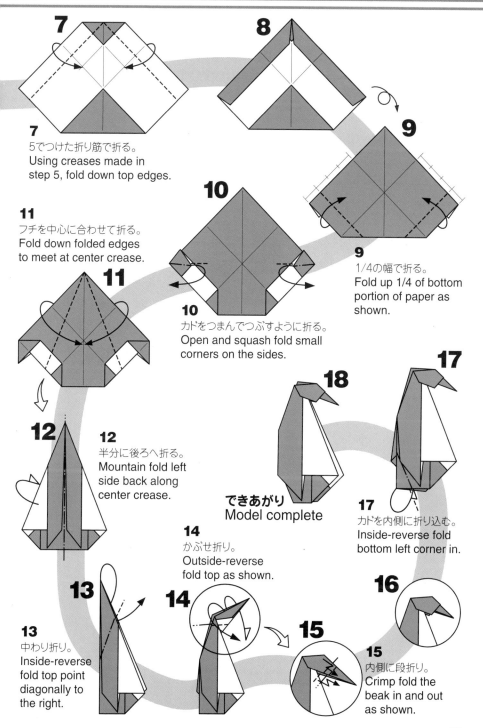

7
5でつけた折り筋で折る。
Using creases made in step 5, fold down top edges.

9
1/4の幅で折る。
Fold up 1/4 of bottom portion of paper as shown.

11
フチを中心に合わせて折る。
Fold down folded edges to meet at center crease.

10
カドをつまんでつぶすように折る。
Open and squash fold small corners on the sides.

12
半分に後ろへ折る。
Mountain fold left side back along center crease.

14
かぶせ折り。
Outside-reverse fold top as shown.

13
中わり折り。
Inside-reverse fold top point diagonally to the right.

15
内側に段折り。
Crimp fold the beak in and out as shown.

17
カドを内側に折り込む。
Inside-reverse fold bottom left corner in.

できあがり
Model complete

71

エンゼル フィッシュ
ANGELFISH

カラー口絵Page15

ラッピングペーパーなどカラフ ルな紙を使って、きれいな魚を 作りましょう。

Fold this model from wrapping paper or other colorful print paper for beautiful results.

紙·Paper Dimension
大/Large: 6cm×6cm···1
小/Small: 5cm×5cm···1

6

フチを折り筋に合わせて 折り筋をつける。
Fold raw edges to the center crease on top and bottom flaps and unfold.

7

カドとカドを合わせて 内側をひろげて つぶすように折る。
Petal fold corners to the center point matching circles.

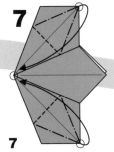

5

内側をひろげて つぶすように折る。
Open top layers of paper and squash fold corners evenly.

4

フチとフチを合わせて 折り筋をつける。
Fold center folded edges to the left folded edges and unfold.

1

三角に折り筋をつける。
White side up, fold in half diagonally and unfold.

2

三角に折る。
Fold in half both ways.

3

カドとカドを 合わせて折る。
Fold top and bottom corners to the right corner.

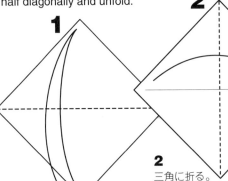

8

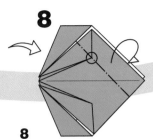

8

○のところで上の1枚を
内側に折る。
Mountain fold top layer
behind from circle point.

9

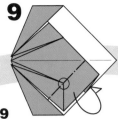

9

○のところで上の1枚を
内側に折る。
Mountain fold top layer
behind from circle point.

10

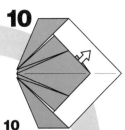

10

カドを引き出して
つまむように折る。
Pull out corner from
inside model and fold flat.

15

カドを引き出して
つまむように折る。
Pull out corner
hidden inside and
flatten.

15

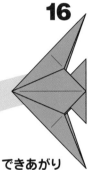

16

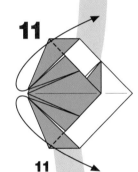

できあがり
Model complete

11

カドを反対側に折る。
Fold flaps out, top
and bottom.

11

14

14

同じように上の
フチのところで
内側に折る。
Fold top raw edge down
and tuck under top layer.

13

13

上のフチのところで
内側に折る。
Fold bottom right edge up
and tuck under top layer.

12

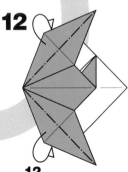

12

カドを後ろへ折る。
Mountain fold flaps
behind.

ちょうちょ
BUTTERFLY

カラー口絵Page14

薄い紙で折るとかわいいちょう
ちょに仕上がります。

Folded out of thin paper,
this butterfly is beautiful.

紙・Paper Dimension
15cm×15cm・・・1

6
少しカドが出るように
折る。
Fold bottom corner up
slightly past top raw edges.

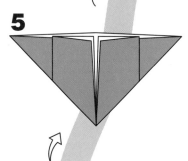

5

4
フチとフチを合わせて
三角に折る。
Fold up both folded
corners to the top
edge to meet.

3

1
半分に折る。
Colored side up, fold
paper in half.

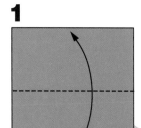

2
上の1枚だけ半分に折る。
Fold top layer only
down to the bottom
folded edge.

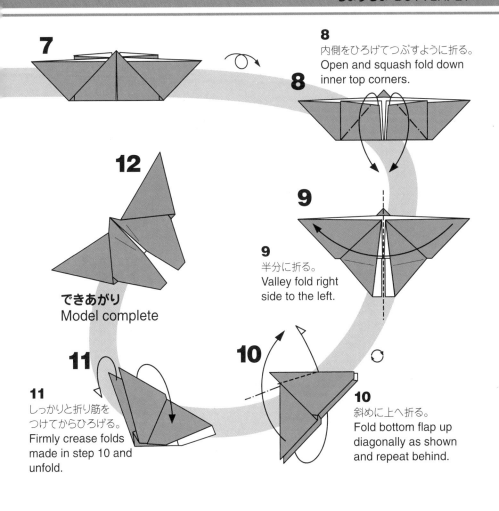

7

8
内側をひろげてつぶすように折る。
Open and squash fold down
inner top corners.

8

9
半分に折る。
Valley fold right
side to the left.

9

12

できあがり
Model complete

11

10

10
斜めに上へ折る。
Fold bottom flap up
diagonally as shown
and repeat behind.

11
しっかりと折り筋を
つけてからひろげる。
Firmly crease folds
made in step 10 and
unfold.

せ み
CICADA

カラー口絵Page14

2種類のせみを紹介します。色や大きさを変えて作ってみましょう。

Here are two kinds of cicada. Experiment folding from different colors and sizes to see the results.

紙·Paper Dimension

15cm×15cm···1

6
フチを少し折る。
Roll down narrow pleat as shown.

6

せみ2/Cicada 2

5
上の1枚だけ下に折る。
Fold down corner of top layer only.

5

4
カドを斜め下に折る。
Fold down top corners at slight angle.

4

3
カドとカドを合わせて折る。
Fold bottom corners to the top corner.

3

1

2

1
三角に折り筋をつける。
White side up, fold in half diagonally and unfold.

2
三角に折る。
Fold bottom corner up to the top.

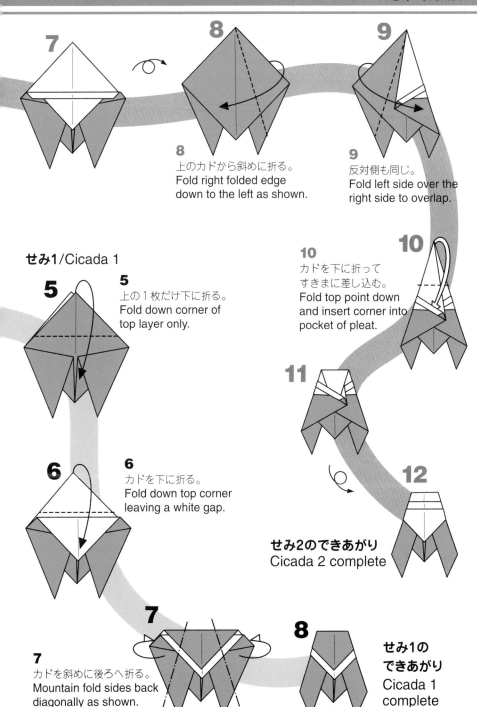

8
上のカドから斜めに折る。
Fold right folded edge down to the left as shown.

9
反対側も同じ。
Fold left side over the right side to overlap.

せみ1/Cicada 1

5
上の1枚だけ下に折る。
Fold down corner of top layer only.

6
カドを下に折る。
Fold down top corner leaving a white gap.

7
カドを斜めに後ろへ折る。
Mountain fold sides back diagonally as shown.

10
カドを下に折って
すきまに差し込む。
Fold top point down and insert corner into pocket of pleat.

せみ2のできあがり
Cicada 2 complete

せみ1のできあがり
Cicada 1 complete

バッタ

GRASS HOPPER

カラー口絵Page14

足をきれいに折ると、今にもとび上がりそうなバッタができあがります。

Fold the legs carefully and your grasshopper will look like it's ready to jump.

紙・Paper Dimension

15cm×15cm・・・1

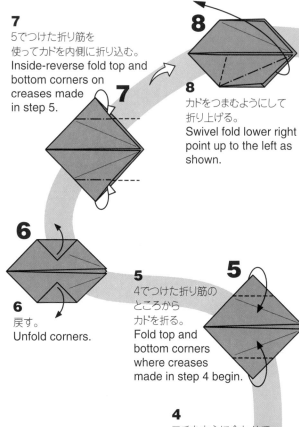

7
5でつけた折り筋を使ってカドを内側に折り込む。
Inside-reverse fold top and bottom corners on creases made in step 5.

8
カドをつまむようにして折り上げる。
Swivel fold lower right point up to the left as shown.

6
戻す。
Unfold corners.

5
4でつけた折り筋のところからカドを折る。
Fold top and bottom corners where creases made in step 4 begin.

4
フチを中心に合わせて折り筋をつける。
Fold raw edges to meet at center crease and unfold.

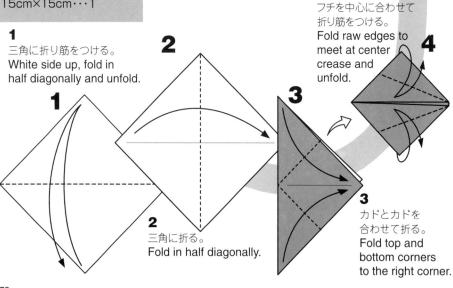

1
三角に折り筋をつける。
White side up, fold in half diagonally and unfold.

2
三角に折る。
Fold in half diagonally.

3
カドとカドを合わせて折る。
Fold top and bottom corners to the right corner.

78

9
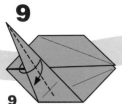

9
半分に折り筋をつける。
Valley fold point in
half and unfold.

10
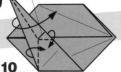

10
9でつけた折り筋でつまんで
カドを細く折る。
Swivel fold point to the
right using crease made
in step 9.

11

11
反対側も同じ。
Repeat steps 8-10
on upper flap.

12
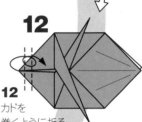

12
カドを
巻くように折る。
Fold in small corner
on left corner and roll over.

13

13
カドを後ろへ折る。
Mountain fold right
corner behind as shown.

14
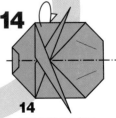

14
半分に後ろへ折る。
Mountain fold model
in half lengthwise.

15

15
カドとカドを
結ぶ線で内側へ折り込む。
Mountain fold corner to the inside from
point to point as shown. Repeat behind.

16
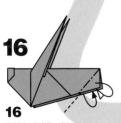

16
カドを内側へ折る。
Mountain fold in
corners to form
point.

17

17
内側へ折る。
Mountain fold in
corners to form
point.

18

18
中わり折り。反対側も同じ。
Inside-reverse fold top
point down to make rear
leg and repeat behind.

19

19
中わり折り。反対側も同じ。
Inside-reverse fold
points of legs to form
feet and repeat behind.

20

できあがり
Model complete

79

コアラ
KOALA

カラー口絵Page14

紙の大きさを変えて、親子のコ
アラを作ってもいいですね。

Using two different sized
papers, try folding a
mother and baby koala.

紙・Paper Dimension
15cm×15cm···3

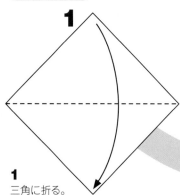

6
カドのところから
斜めに折る。
Fold up bottom left
edges diagonally.

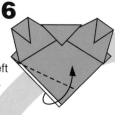

5
カドを下に折る。
Fold down point
between ears.

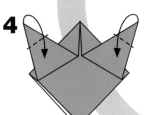

4
カドを少し折る。
Fold down corners
a little.

3
カドを斜めに上に折る。
Fold points up and
out diagonally.

かお／Face

1
三角に折る。
White side up, fold
in half diagonally.

2
カドとカドを
合わせて折る。
Fold points down
to the bottom point.

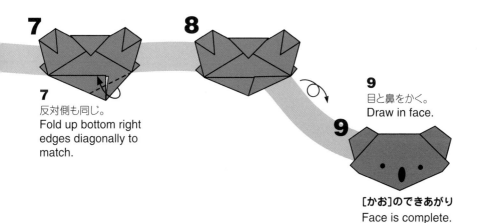

7

7

反対側も同じ。
Fold up bottom right
edges diagonally to
match.

8

9

目と鼻をかく。
Draw in face.

[かお]のできあがり
Face is complete.

からだ／ **Body**

紙を2枚使う。
Uses two sheets
of paper.

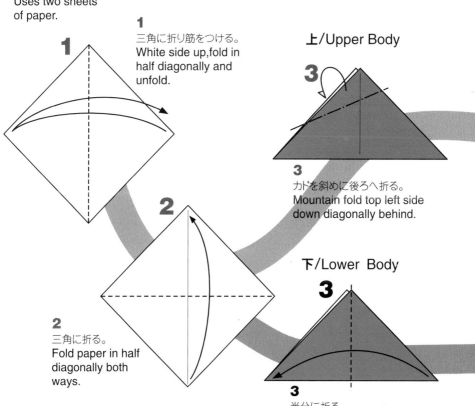

1

三角に折り筋をつける。
White side up,fold in
half diagonally and
unfold.

1

2

三角に折る。
Fold paper in half
diagonally both
ways.

2

上/Upper Body

3

3

カドを斜めに後ろへ折る。
Mountain fold top left side
down diagonally behind.

下/Lower Body

3

3

半分に折る。
Fold right corner to the left.

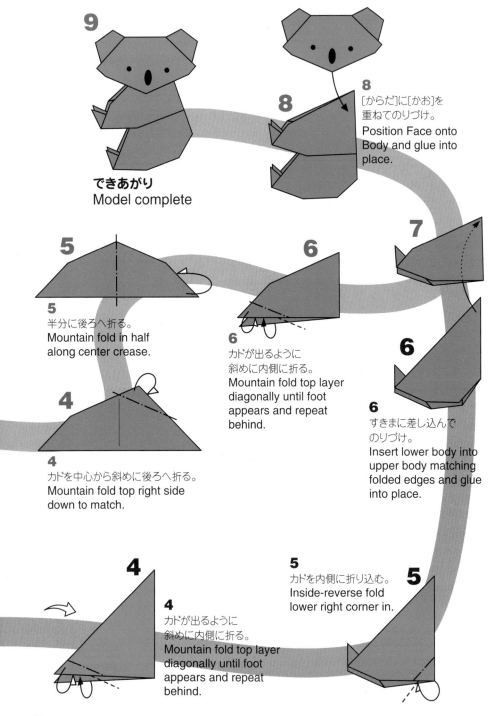

9

できあがり
Model complete

8

8
[からだ]に[かお]を
重ねてのりづけ。
Position Face onto
Body and glue into
place.

7

5

5
半分に後ろへ折る。
Mountain fold in half
along center crease.

4
カドを中心から斜めに後ろへ折る。
Mountain fold top right side
down to match.

6

6
カドが出るように
斜めに内側に折る。
Mountain fold top layer
diagonally until foot
appears and repeat
behind.

6

6
すきまに差し込んで
のりづけ。
Insert lower body into
upper body matching
folded edges and glue
into place.

4

4
カドが出るように
斜めに内側に折る。
Mountain fold top layer
diagonally until foot
appears and repeat
behind.

5
カドを内側に折り込む。
Inside-reverse fold
lower right corner in.

5

パンダ

PANDA

カラー口絵Page14

目と鼻は、自由にかき込んで、かわいいパンダを作りましょう。

Drawing in eyes and a nose, you can create a really cute panda.

紙·Paper Dimension

15cm×15cm···3

かお／ Face

1

三角に
折り筋をつける。
Colored side up, fold in half diagonally and unfold.

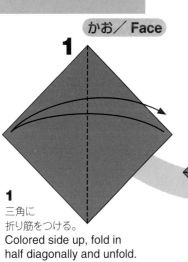

2

三角に折る。
Fold in half diagonally crosswise.

3

カドとカドを合わせて折る。
Fold points down to the bottom point.

4

カドとカドを
合わせて折る。
Fold points at the bottom to the top.

5

カドとカドを
合わせて折る。
Fold points at the top out to the side corners.

6

内側をひろげて
つぶすように折る。
Open and squash fold small flaps evenly as shown.

7

カドを少し折る。
Fold side corners slightly in.

83

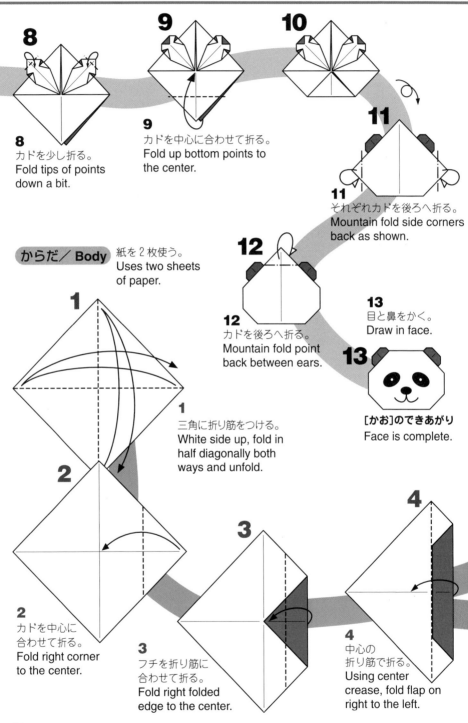

8

8
カドを少し折る。
Fold tips of points
down a bit.

9
カドを中心に合わせて折る。
Fold up bottom points to
the center.

10

11
それぞれカドを後ろへ折る。
Mountain fold side corners
back as shown.

12
カドを後ろへ折る。
Mountain fold point
back between ears.

13
目と鼻をかく。
Draw in face.

13

[かお]のできあがり
Face is complete.

からだ／ Body 紙を2枚使う。
Uses two sheets
of paper.

1

1
三角に折り筋をつける。
White side up, fold in
half diagonally both
ways and unfold.

2

2
カドを中心に
合わせて折る。
Fold right corner
to the center.

3

3
フチを折り筋に
合わせて折る。
Fold right folded
edge to the center.

4

4
中心の
折り筋で折る。
Using center
crease, fold flap on
right to the left.

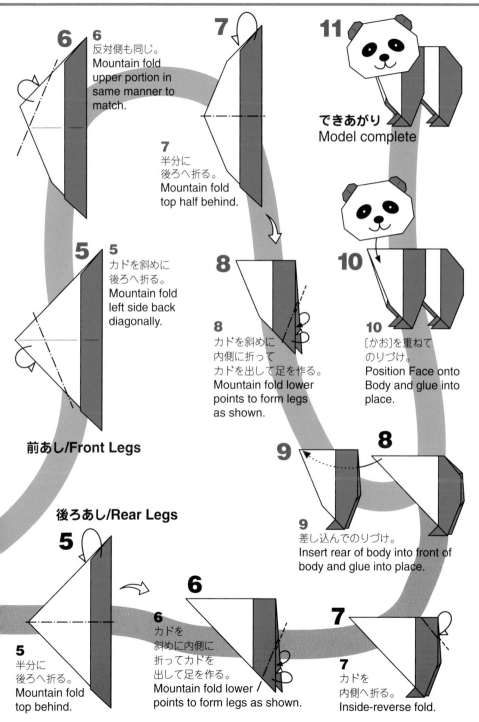

6

反対側も同じ。
Mountain fold upper portion in same manner to match.

7

半分に
後ろへ折る。
Mountain fold top half behind.

11

できあがり
Model complete

5

カドを斜めに
後ろへ折る。
Mountain fold left side back diagonally.

8

カドを斜めに
内側に折って
カドを出して足を作る。
Mountain fold lower points to form legs as shown.

10

［かお］を重ねて
のりづけ。
Position Face onto Body and glue into place.

前あし/Front Legs

9

差し込んでのりづけ。
Insert rear of body into front of body and glue into place.

8

後ろあし/Rear Legs

5

半分に
後ろへ折る。
Mountain fold top behind.

6

カドを
斜めに内側に
折ってカドを
出して足を作る。
Mountain fold lower points to form legs as shown.

7

カドを
内側へ折る。
Inside-reverse fold.

ライオン

LION

カラー口絵Page14

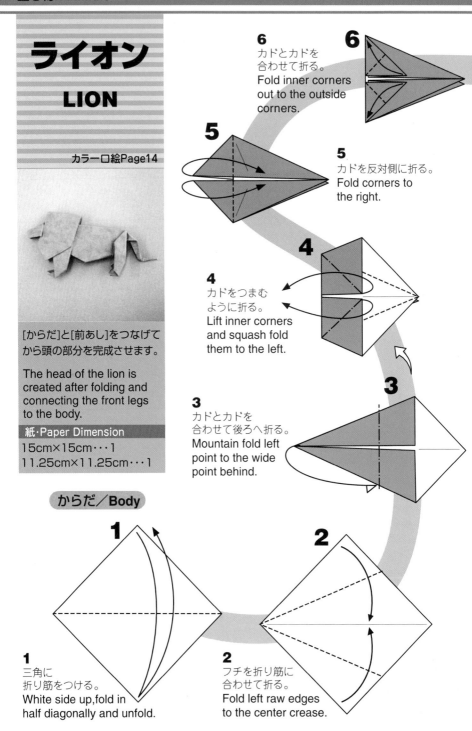

[からだ]と[前あし]をつなげて
から頭の部分を完成させます。

The head of the lion is
created after folding and
connecting the front legs
to the body.

紙·Paper Dimension

15cm×15cm···1
11.25cm×11.25cm···1

6

カドとカドを
合わせて折る。
Fold inner corners
out to the outside
corners.

6

5

5

カドを反対側に折る。
Fold corners to
the right.

4

4

カドをつまむ
ように折る。
Lift inner corners
and squash fold
them to the left.

3

3

カドとカドを
合わせて後ろへ折る。
Mountain fold left
point to the wide
point behind.

からだ／Body

1

1

三角に
折り筋をつける。
White side up,fold in
half diagonally and unfold.

2

2

フチを折り筋に
合わせて折る。
Fold left raw edges
to the center crease.

86

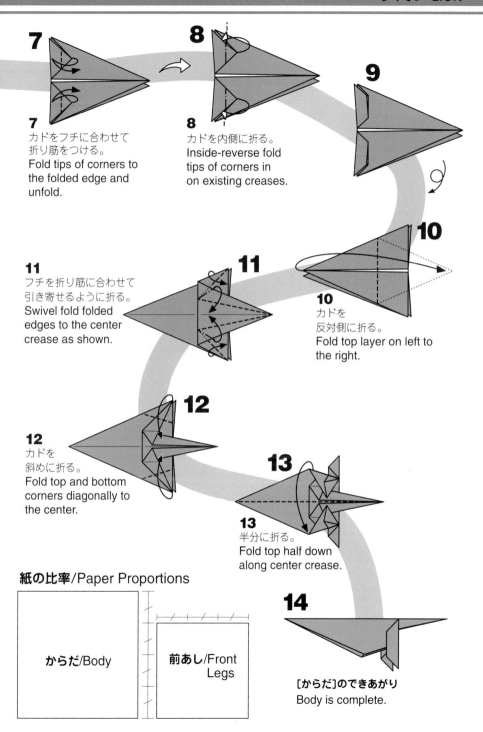

7

7
カドをフチに合わせて
折り筋をつける。
Fold tips of corners to
the folded edge and
unfold.

8

8
カドを内側に折る。
Inside-reverse fold
tips of corners in
on existing creases.

9

10

10
カドを
反対側に折る。
Fold top layer on left to
the right.

11

11
フチを折り筋に合わせて
引き寄せるように折る。
Swivel fold folded
edges to the center
crease as shown.

12

12
カドを
斜めに折る。
Fold top and bottom
corners diagonally to
the center.

13

13
半分に折る。
Fold top half down
along center crease.

14

[からだ]のできあがり
Body is complete.

紙の比率/Paper Proportions

からだ/Body

前あし/Front
Legs

前あし／Front Legs

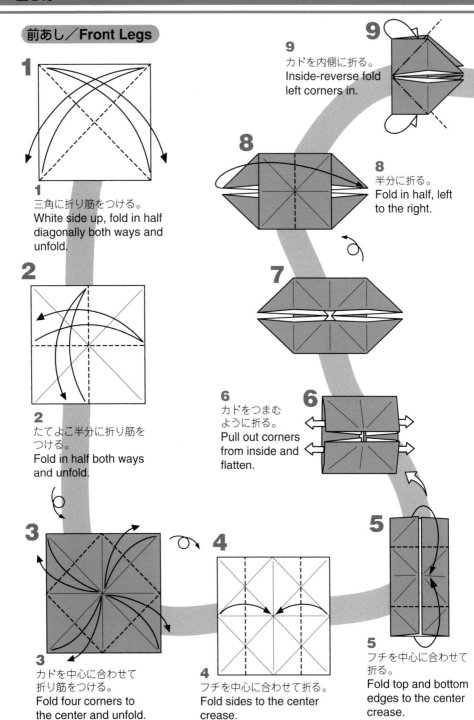

1
三角に折り筋をつける。
White side up, fold in half diagonally both ways and unfold.

2
たてよこ半分に折り筋をつける。
Fold in half both ways and unfold.

3
カドを中心に合わせて折り筋をつける。
Fold four corners to the center and unfold.

4
フチを中心に合わせて折る。
Fold sides to the center crease.

5
フチを中心に合わせて折る。
Fold top and bottom edges to the center crease.

6
カドをつまむように折る。
Pull out corners from inside and flatten.

7

8
半分に折る。
Fold in half, left to the right.

9
カドを内側に折る。
Inside-reverse fold left corners in.

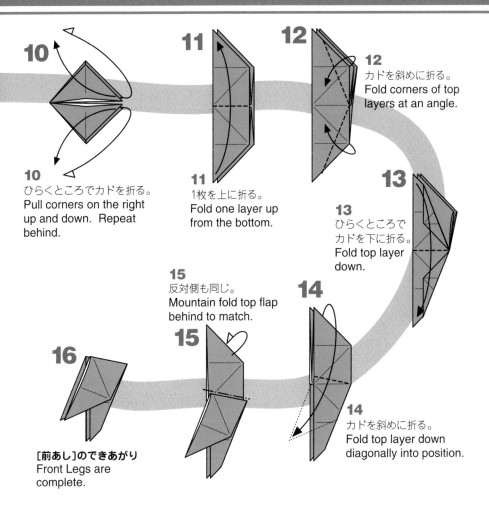

10

10
ひらくところでカドを折る。
Pull corners on the right
up and down. Repeat
behind.

11

11
1枚を上に折る。
Fold one layer up
from the bottom.

12

12
カドを斜めに折る。
Fold corners of top
layers at an angle.

13

13
ひらくところで
カドを下に折る。
Fold top layer
down.

15
反対側も同じ。
Mountain fold top flap
behind to match.

15

14

14
カドを斜めに折る。
Fold top layer down
diagonally into position.

16

[前あし]のできあがり
Front Legs are
complete.

しあげ／ASSEMBLY

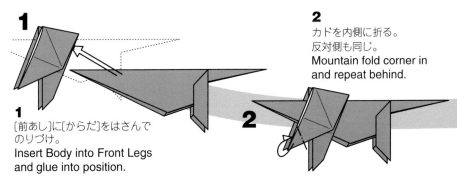

1

1
[前あし]に[からだ]をはさんで
のりづけ。
Insert Body into Front Legs
and glue into position.

2
カドを内側に折る。
反対側も同じ。
Mountain fold corner in
and repeat behind.

2

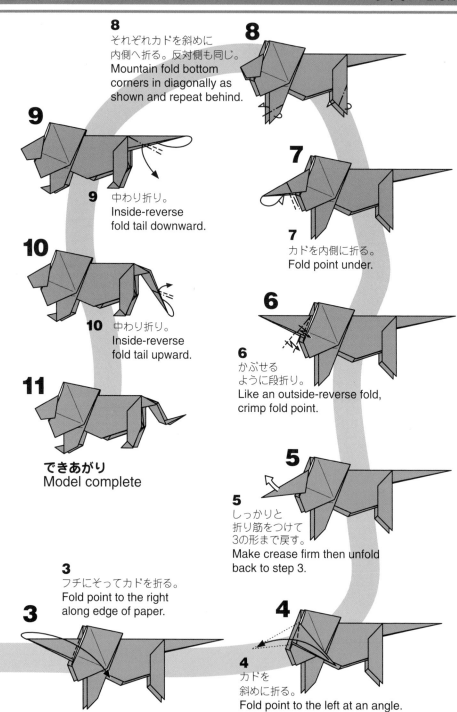

8

それぞれカドを斜めに
内側へ折る。反対側も同じ。
Mountain fold bottom
corners in diagonally as
shown and repeat behind.

9

中わり折り。
Inside-reverse
fold tail downward.

7

カドを内側に折る。
Fold point under.

10

中わり折り。
Inside-reverse
fold tail upward.

6

かぶせる
ように段折り。
Like an outside-reverse fold,
crimp fold point.

11

できあがり
Model complete

5

しっかりと
折り筋をつけて
3の形まで戻す。
Make crease firm then unfold
back to step 3.

3

フチにそってカドを折る。
Fold point to the right
along edge of paper.

4

カドを
斜めに折る。
Fold point to the left at an angle.

ぞう
ELEPHANT

カラー口絵Page14

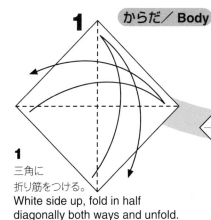

むずかしそうですが、折り筋を
きちんとつけて折っていくのが
コツです。

This model appears
difficult to fold. The secret
to success is to make your
creases firmly and
accurately.

紙・Paper Dimension

15cm×15cm・・・1
11.25cm×11.25cm・・・1

5

引き寄せるように折る。
Swivel fold the top and bottom
raw edges to the center crease
using existing creases.

5

4

4

カドが少し
出るように折る。
Fold right corner
1/3 to the right so
that it protrudes a bit.

3

3

カドを中心に合わせて折る。
Fold top, bottom and
right corners to
the center.

1

からだ／ Body

2

2

フチを折り筋に
合わせて少しだけ
折り筋をつける。
Bring raw edges
to the center
crease but fold
only right half of
paper to crease
corner. Unfold.

1

三角に
折り筋をつける。
White side up, fold in half
diagonally both ways and unfold.

91

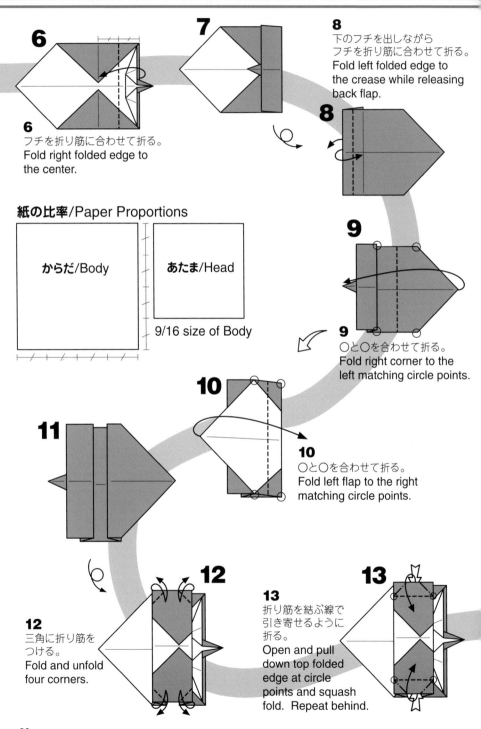

6
フチを折り筋に合わせて折る。
Fold right folded edge to
the center.

7

8
下のフチを出しながら
フチを折り筋に合わせて折る。
Fold left folded edge to
the crease while releasing
back flap.

8

紙の比率/Paper Proportions

からだ/Body

あたま/Head

9/16 size of Body

9
○と○を合わせて折る。
Fold right corner to the
left matching circle points.

10
○と○を合わせて折る。
Fold left flap to the right
matching circle points.

11

12
三角に折り筋を
つける。
Fold and unfold
four corners.

13
折り筋を結ぶ線で
引き寄せるように
折る。
Open and pull
down top folded
edge at circle
points and squash
fold. Repeat behind.

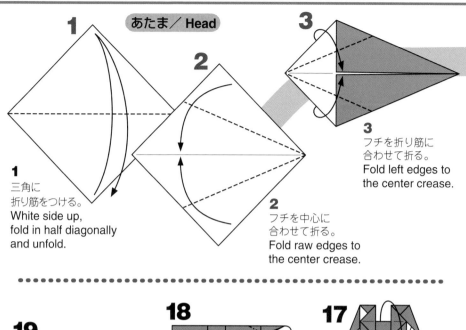

1
あたま／ Head

1
三角に
折り筋をつける。
White side up,
fold in half diagonally
and unfold.

2
フチを中心に
合わせて折る。
Fold raw edges to
the center crease.

3
フチを折り筋に
合わせて折る。
Fold left edges to
the center crease.

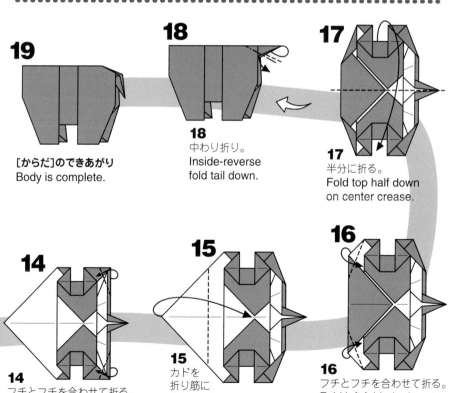

19

[からだ]のできあがり
Body is complete.

18
中わり折り。
Inside-reverse
fold tail down.

17
半分に折る。
Fold top half down
on center crease.

14
フチとフチを合わせて折る。
Fold right folded edges
to lie along triangular folds.

15
カドを
折り筋に
合わせて折る。
Fold left corner to
the center crease.

16
フチとフチを合わせて折る。
Fold left folded edges to
lie along triangular folds.

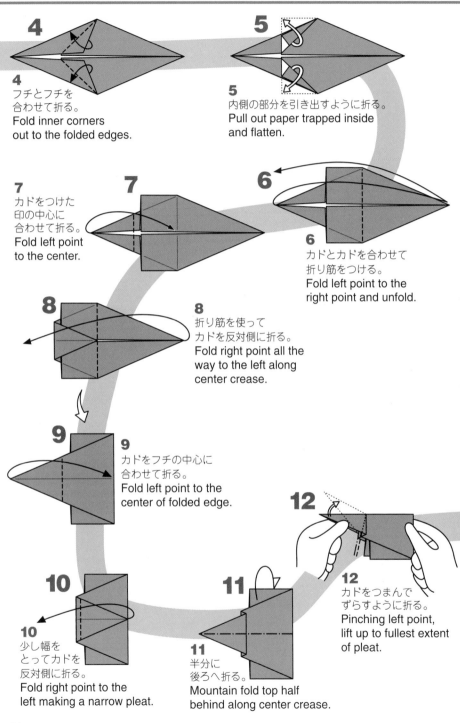

4

4
フチとフチを
合わせて折る。
Fold inner corners
out to the folded edges.

5

5
内側の部分を引き出すように折る。
Pull out paper trapped inside
and flatten.

7
カドをつけた
印の中心に
合わせて折る。
Fold left point
to the center.

7

6

6
カドとカドを合わせて
折り筋をつける。
Fold left point to the
right point and unfold.

8

8
折り筋を使って
カドを反対側に折る。
Fold right point all the
way to the left along
center crease.

9

9
カドをフチの中心に
合わせて折る。
Fold left point to the
center of folded edge.

12

12
カドをつまんで
ずらすように折る。
Pinching left point,
lift up to fullest extent
of pleat.

10

10
少し幅を
とってカドを
反対側に折る。
Fold right point to the
left making a narrow pleat.

11

11
半分に
後ろへ折る。
Mountain fold top half
behind along center crease.

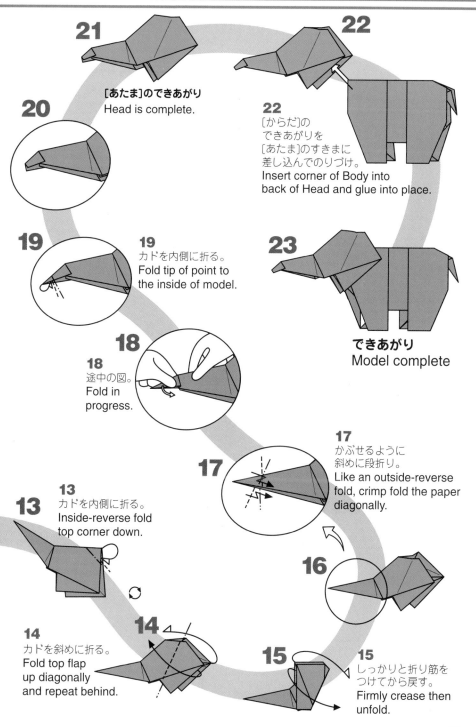

21

20

[あたま]のできあがり
Head is complete.

22

22
[からだ]の
できあがりを
[あたま]のすきまに
差し込んでのりづけ。
Insert corner of Body into
back of Head and glue into place.

19

19
カドを内側に折る。
Fold tip of point to
the inside of model.

23

できあがり
Model complete

18

18
途中の図。
Fold in
progress.

17

17
かぶせるように
斜めに段折り。
Like an outside-reverse
fold, crimp fold the paper
diagonally.

13

13
カドを内側に折る。
Inside-reverse fold
top corner down.

16

14

14
カドを斜めに折る。
Fold top flap
up diagonally
and repeat behind.

15

15
しっかりと折り筋を
つけてから戻す。
Firmly crease then
unfold.

ネコの しおり
BOOKMARK CAT

カラー口絵Page9

かわいいネコのしおりです。本をプレゼントするときにつけてあげましょう。

This is a cute cat bookmark. When giving a book, include this bookmark with your gift.

紙・Paper Dimension

15cm×7.5cm・・・1

6

フチを中心に合わせて折る。上のカドは内側に折る。
Fold left side to the center and inside-reverse fold top left corner.

6

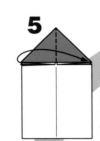
5

5

上の1枚のカドを反対側に折る。
Fold left corner flap to the right.

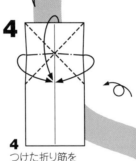
4

4

つけた折り筋を使って折りたたむ。
Using existing creases, collapse the top edge down.

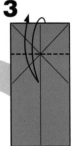
3

3

折り筋の交点のところで折り筋をつける。
Fold top edge down through intersection of existing creases and unfold.

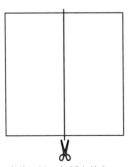

半分に切った紙を使う。
Cut and use half of square a paper.

1

1

半分に折り筋をつける。
White side up, fold left side to the right and unfold.

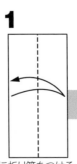

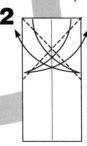
2

2

フチとフチを合わせて折り筋をつける。
Fold top edge down to the left edge and unfold. Then fold top edge down to the right edge and unfold.

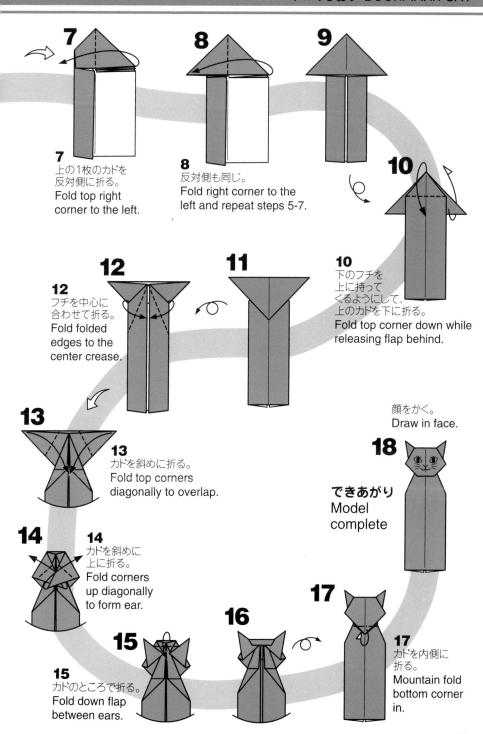

7
上の1枚のカドを
反対側に折る。
Fold top right
corner to the left.

8
反対側も同じ。
Fold right corner to the
left and repeat steps 5-7.

10
下のフチを
上に持って
くるようにして、
上のカドを下に折る。
Fold top corner down while
releasing flap behind.

12
フチを中心に
合わせて折る。
Fold folded
edges to the
center crease.

13
カドを斜めに折る。
Fold top corners
diagonally to overlap.

14
カドを斜めに
上に折る。
Fold corners
up diagonally
to form ear.

15
カドのところで折る。
Fold down flap
between ears.

17
カドを内側に
折る。
Mountain fold
bottom corner
in.

顔をかく。
Draw in face.

18

できあがり
Model
complete

ハートの しおり
BOOKMARK HEART

カラー口絵Page9

かんたんに作れるハートの作品
です。紙の裏表で色の違う紙を
使うといいですよ。

This is an easy heart to
make. Use paper that has
different colored sides for
best results.

紙·Paper Dimension

15cm×7.5cm···1

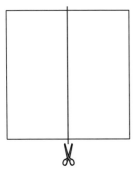

半分に切った紙を使う。
Cut and use half of
square a paper.

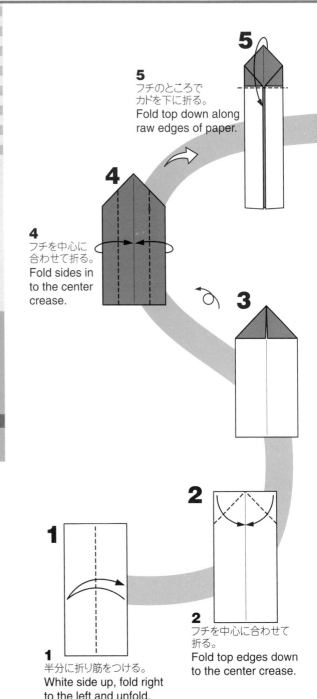

5
フチのところで
カドを下に折る。
Fold top down along
raw edges of paper.

4
フチを中心に
合わせて折る。
Fold sides in
to the center
crease.

2
フチを中心に合わせて
折る。
Fold top edges down
to the center crease.

1
半分に折り筋をつける。
White side up, fold right
to the left and unfold.

6

7

7
カドから1/3のところで
斜めに折り筋をつける。
Fold top corners down
about 1/3 and unfold.

8

8
カドを内側に
折る。
Inside-reverse
fold corners in.

9

9
カドを少し内側に折る。
Mountain fold inner
corners behind.

10

11

11
フチをカドのところで
折る。
Fold sides in from
corner points at top
to narrow.

12

13

できあがり
Model complete

さくらの器

CHERRY BLOSSOM CONTAINER

カラー口絵Page2

5枚の花びらをつなぎ合わせるとかわいい桜の花になります。お菓子皿としても使えます。

Connecting five petals together, you can make a nice cherry blossom. Using it as a container, you can place candies and other small items in it.

紙・Paper Dimension

5cm×10cm・・・5

半分に切った紙を使う。
Cut square into half.

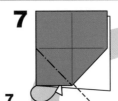

7
6でつけた折り筋を使ってカドを内側に折り込む。
Using creases made in step 6, inside-reverse fold corner in.

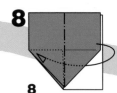

8
フチを内側のカドにかぶせるように折る。
Mountain fold top flap back to cover corner inside.

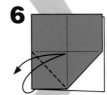

6
カドを中心に合わせて折り筋をつける。
Fold bottom left corner to the center and unfold.

5
半分に折る。
Refold left to the right on center crease.

4
フチを3でつけた折り筋に合わせて折る。
Fold up bottom left corner to the crease made in step 3.

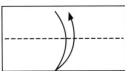

1
半分に折り筋をつける。
White side up, fold paper in half lengthwise and unfold.

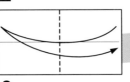

2
半分に折り筋をつける。
Fold right edge to the left edge and unfold.

3
フチを中心に合わせて折り筋をつける。
Fold left edge to the center crease and unfold.

100

9

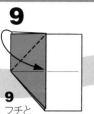

9
フチと
フチを合わせて折る。
Fold top left corner
to the center crease.

10

10
半分に後ろへ折る。
Mountain fold bottom
side behind along
center crease.

11

11
フチとフチを合わせて
折り筋をつける。
Fold bottom right corner to
the top center and unfold.

12

12
フチを11の
折り筋に合わせて
折り筋をつける。
Fold bottom right folded edge
to the crease made in step 11.

13

13
フチを12の折り筋に
合わせて折る。
Fold outer corner raw
edges to the crease
made in step 12.

14

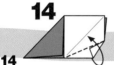

14
12でつけた折り筋で折る。
Refold right flap up on
creases made in step 12.

15

15
同じものを5つ作る。
Make 5 petals
like this.

16

16
☆のカドをすきまに
差し込んで
かるくのりづけ。
Insert corner flap
marked with ☆ into
pocket of another
petal and glue
lightly into place.

17

17
同じようにして
5つつなげる。
In same manner,
connect the
remaining petals.

18

18
ハシとハシを持って
ひろげる。
Grasp outer edges of
front and back petals
and spread open.

20

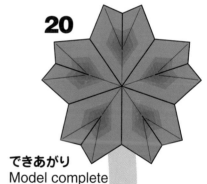

できあがり
Model complete

19

19
残りのカドも同じようにして
すきまに差し込んでのりづけ。
Repeat step 16 with remaining
flaps to close the blossom.

とりの入れ物
BIRD SHAPED CONTAINER
カラー口絵Page11

テーブル上の小物として、厚手の紙で大きく折ってナプキン入れなどに使っても良いでしょう。

For use as a table setting decoration, it is best to use large, sturdy paper to make a model large enough to hold napkins, etc.

紙・Paper Dimension

20cm×20cm···1

6
カドを直角に折り上げてしっかりと折り筋をつける。
Fold bottom right corner up along edge at 90° angle and unfold.

6

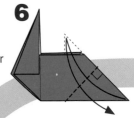

5

5
フチとフチを合わせて折る。
Fold top left raw edge to the vertical folded edge and repeat behind.

4

4
○と○を結ぶ線で中わり折り。
Inside-reverse fold left corner up from circled point to point as shown.

3

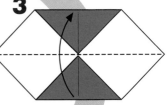

3
半分に折る。
Fold bottom up to the top folded edge.

1

2

1
三角に折り筋をつける。
White side up, fold in half diagonally both ways and unfold.

2
カドを中心に折る。
Fold top and bottom corners to the center point.

102

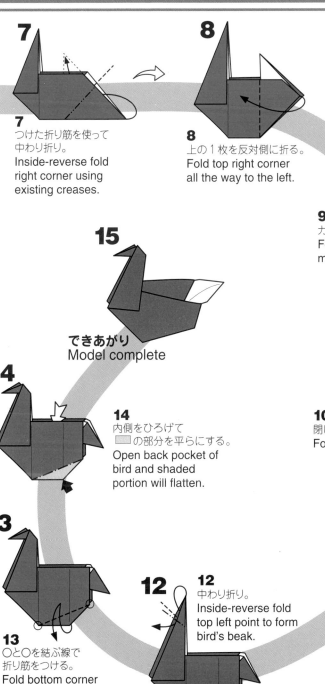

7

つけた折り筋を使って
中わり折り。
Inside-reverse fold
right corner using
existing creases.

8

上の1枚を反対側に折る。
Fold top right corner
all the way to the left.

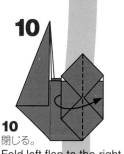

9

カドを中心に合わせて折る。
Fold outer corners to
meet at center crease.

10

閉じる。
Fold left flap to the right.

11

中わり折り。
Inside-reverse fold
small flap on right to
fullest extent.

12

中わり折り。
Inside-reverse fold
top left point to form
bird's beak.

13

○と○を結ぶ線で
折り筋をつける。
Fold bottom corner
up between circle
points and unfold.

14

内側をひろげて
▭の部分を平らにする。
Open back pocket of
bird and shaded
portion will flatten.

15

できあがり
Model complete

ナイフ&フォーク ホルダー
KNIFE & FORK HOLDER

カラー口絵Page11

パーティーのときなどに大活躍する作品です。紙の種類や色を変えるとおしゃれです。

At parties, this model is very useful. Depending upon the occasion, you can change the color and pattern of the paper for a wonderful effect.

紙・Paper Dimension
15cm×15cm・・・1

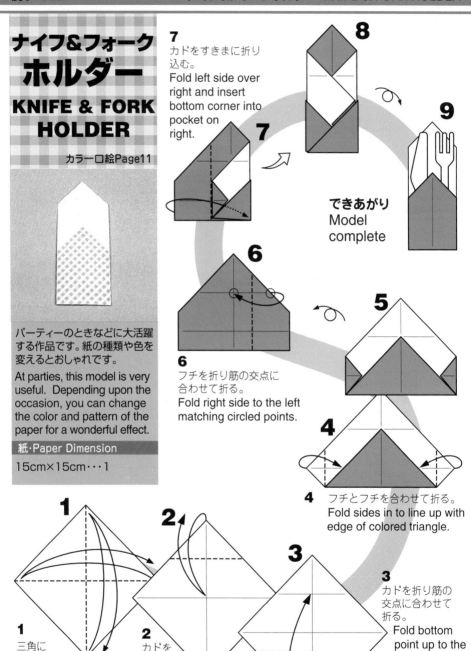

7
カドをすきまに折り込む。
Fold left side over right and insert bottom corner into pocket on right.

8

9

できあがり
Model complete

6
フチを折り筋の交点に合わせて折る。
Fold right side to the left matching circled points.

5

4
フチとフチを合わせて折る。
Fold sides in to line up with edge of colored triangle.

3
カドを折り筋の交点に合わせて折る。
Fold bottom point up to the crease made in step 2.

1
三角に折り筋をつける。
White side up, fold in half diagonally both ways and unfold.

2
カドを中心に合わせて折り筋をつける。
Fold top corner down to the center and unfold.

はしおき

CHOPSTICK REST

カラー口絵Page11

千代紙など色々な柄で折ってみ
ましょう。平らになる部分が均一
になるように注意して下さい。

Try folding this model from
Japanese chiyogami paper
or other print patterned
paper. Carefully fold the base of the
model so that it lies evenly
on the table.

紙・Paper Dimension
7.5cm×15cm···1

半分に切った紙を使う。
Cut square into half.

割りばしの袋を使って折ることも
できる。はし袋で折るときは4から折る。
You can also fold this model from
chopstick wrappers. When folding
chopstick wrappers, begin folding
from step 4.

9

できあがり
Model complete

8

8
途中の図。
Fold in progress.

7
すきまに指を入れてひろげながら、
黒矢印のところをつぶして平らに
するように立体的にする。
Open up model at center bottom
and shape top with rounded
mountain crease as shown.

7

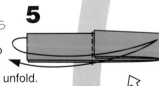

6
つけた折り筋でフチを
一方のすきまに差し込む。
Insert left side deeply
into pocket of right.

6

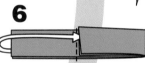

5
フチのところから
折り筋をつける。
Fold left side to
the right along
raw edges and unfold.

5

4

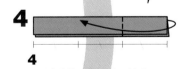

4
フチを1/3のところで折る。
Fold right edge 1/3 to the left.

1

1
折り筋をつける。
White side up,
fold top down
to the bottom
and unfold.

2

2
フチを中心に
合わせて折る。
Fold raw edges
to the center crease.

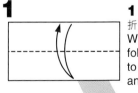

3

3
半分に折る。
Fold top half
down.

105

ハートの
ナプキンリング
HEART
SHAPED
NAPKIN RING

カラー口絵Page10

メンバーに合わせて色を変えて
作れば、テーブルが華やかにな
りますね。

If you want to separate your
guests, you can use different
colored napkin rings and
make a colorful table setting.

紙・Paper Dimension

15cm×7.5cm···1

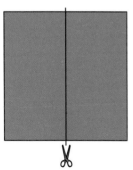

半分に切った紙を使う。
Cut and use half of
square a paper.

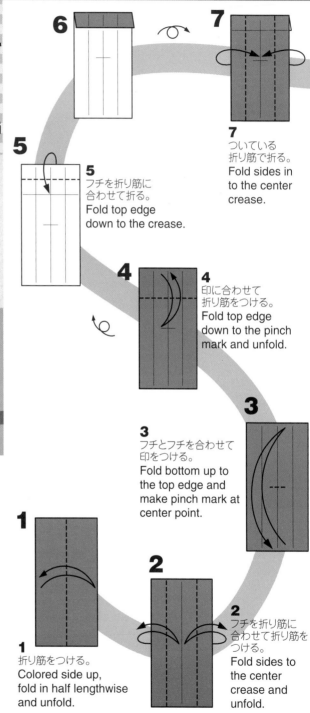

6

7

7
ついている
折り筋で折る。
Fold sides in
to the center
crease.

5

5
フチを折り筋に
合わせて折る。
Fold top edge
down to the crease.

4

4
印に合わせて
折り筋をつける。
Fold top edge
down to the pinch
mark and unfold.

3
フチとフチを合わせて
印をつける。
Fold bottom up to
the top edge and
make pinch mark at
center point.

1

1
折り筋をつける。
Colored side up,
fold in half lengthwise
and unfold.

2

2
フチを折り筋に
合わせて折り筋を
つける。
Fold sides to
the center
crease and
unfold.

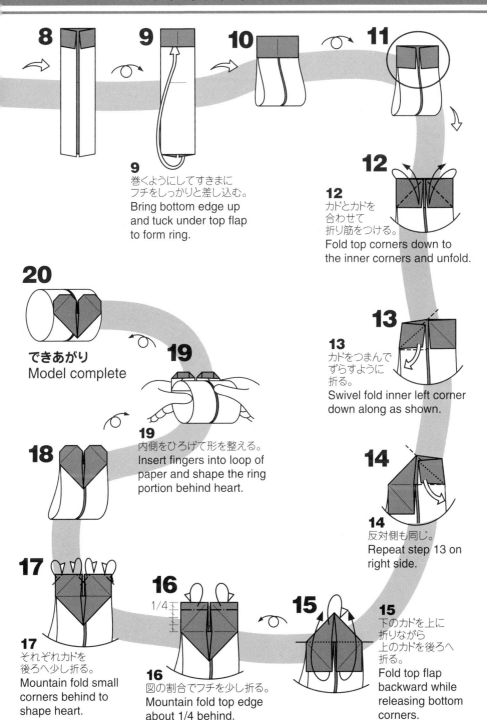

8

9

10

11

9
巻くようにしてすきまに
フチをしっかりと差し込む。
Bring bottom edge up
and tuck under top flap
to form ring.

12
カドとカドを
合わせて
折り筋をつける。
Fold top corners down to
the inner corners and unfold.

13
カドをつまんで
ずらすように
折る。
Swivel fold inner left corner
down along as shown.

14
反対側も同じ。
Repeat step 13 on
right side.

15
下のカドを上に
折りながら
上のカドを後ろへ
折る。
Fold top flap
backward while
releasing bottom
corners.

16
1/4
図の割合でフチを少し折る。
Mountain fold top edge
about 1/4 behind.

17
それぞれカドを
後ろへ少し折る。
Mountain fold small
corners behind to
shape heart.

18

19
内側をひろげて形を整える。
Insert fingers into loop of
paper and shape the ring
portion behind heart.

20
できあがり
Model complete

107

コースター

COASTER

カラー口絵Page8,10

水に強い紙を使いましょう。おしゃれでとても便利なコースターです。

Fold this model from paper that is water-resistant for best results. It is an attractive and practical model.

紙・Paper Dimension

15cm×15cm・・・1 or 2

7

上のフチを後ろへ
下のフチを手前に
折り筋に合わせて折る。
Mountain fold top edge behind to the center crease. Valley fold bottom edge up to the center crease.

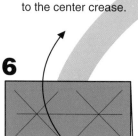

6

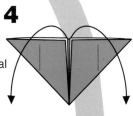

ひろげる。
Open up top layer.

5

反対側も同じ。
Fold top edges down to meet at center and unfold.

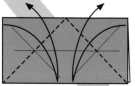

4

しっかりと折り筋を
つけてから戻す。
Firmly crease diagonal edges and unfold.

1

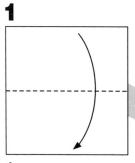

半分に折る。
White side up, fold paper in half.

2

半分に折り筋をつける。
Fold top edge down to the bottom and unfold.

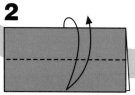

3

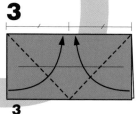

フチとフチを合わせて折る。
Fold up raw edges to meet at center of folded edge.

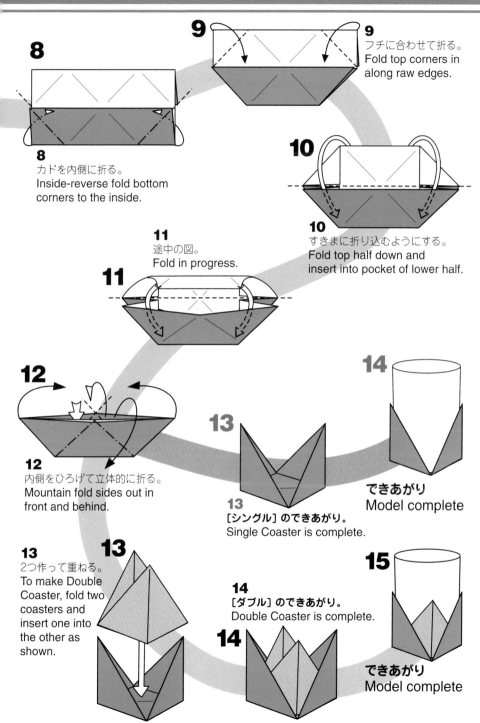

8
カドを内側に折る。
Inside-reverse fold bottom
corners to the inside.

9
フチに合わせて折る。
Fold top corners in
along raw edges.

10
すきまに折り込むようにする。
Fold top half down and
insert into pocket of lower half.

11
途中の図。
Fold in progress.

12
内側をひろげて立体的に折る。
Mountain fold sides out in
front and behind.

13
[シングル] のできあがり。
Single Coaster is complete.

14
できあがり
Model complete

13
2つ作って重ねる。
To make Double
Coaster, fold two
coasters and
insert one into
the other as
shown.

14
[ダブル] のできあがり。
Double Coaster is complete.

15
できあがり
Model complete

なべしき

POT HOLDER

カラー口絵Page8

紙の色や柄を変えると組み合わせが楽しめます。厚手の紙で折るとよいでしょう。

Varying the colors and patterns, you can enjoy the results when you connect the units. It is best to use sturdy paper for this model.

紙・Paper Dimension

11cm×11cm…16

1
三角に折る。
Colored side up, fold in half diagonally.

2
三角に折る。
Fold left corner to the right.

3
内側をひろげてつぶすように折る。
Open top layer and squash fold bottom right corner to the top.

4

5
カドを反対側に折る。
Fold left flap all the way to the right.

6
内側をひろげてつぶすように折る。
Open top layer and squash fold bottom right corner to the top.

7
カドを反対側に折る。
Fold top right flap to the left.

8
折り筋をつける。
Fold top layer down to the bottom and unfold.

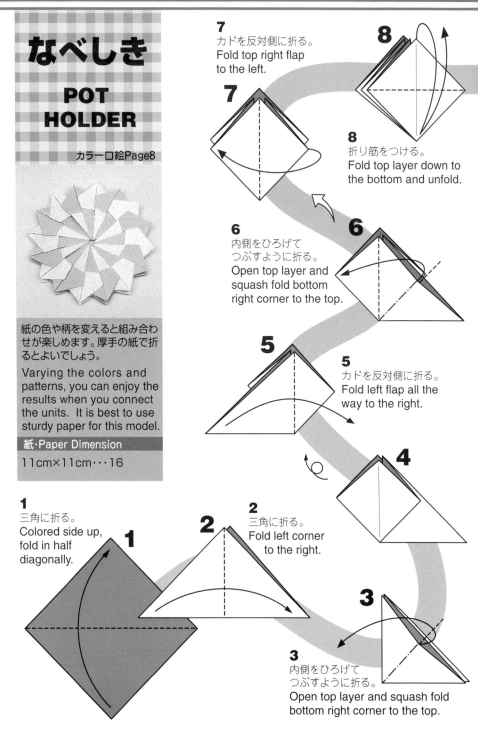

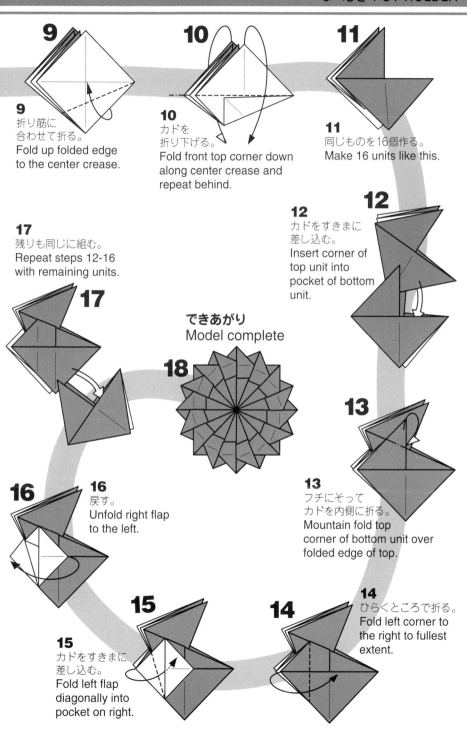

9
折り筋に
合わせて折る。
Fold up folded edge
to the center crease.

10
カドを
折り下げる。
Fold front top corner down
along center crease and
repeat behind.

11
同じものを16個作る。
Make 16 units like this.

12
カドをすきまに
差し込む。
Insert corner of
top unit into
pocket of bottom
unit.

13
フチにそって
カドを内側に折る。
Mountain fold top
corner of bottom unit over
folded edge of top.

14
ひらくところで折る。
Fold left corner to
the right to fullest
extent.

15
カドをすきまに
差し込む。
Fold left flap
diagonally into
pocket on right.

16
戻す。
Unfold right flap
to the left.

17
残りも同じに組む。
Repeat steps 12-16
with remaining units.

できあがり
Model complete

さいふ
WALLET

カラー口絵Page6

折り図通りの大きさで折ると、実用のサイズに折り上がります。和紙や布で折ってみて下さい。
This wallet is practical because careful consideration was made to accommodate various currencies. Following the directions, try folding one for yourself.

紙・Paper Dimension
61cm×43.5cm···1

6
フチを少し折る。
Fold sides in 3cm, noting dimensions.

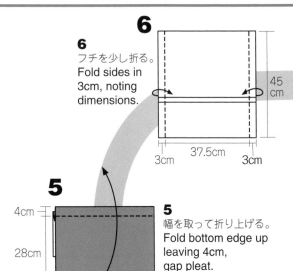

45 cm

3cm   37.5cm   3cm

5

4cm

28cm

5
幅を取って折り上げる。
Fold bottom edge up leaving 4cm, gap pleat.

4
幅を取って折り下げる。
Fold top edge down leaving 6cm, gap pleat.

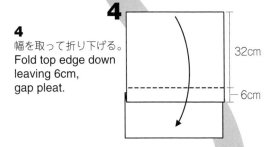

32cm

6cm

1

43.5cm

38cm

23cm

1
図の割合で折る。
Colored side up, fold bottom up as shown.

2

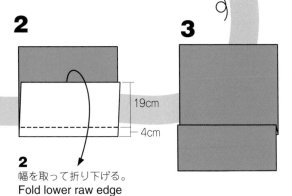

19cm

4cm

2
幅を取って折り下げる。
Fold lower raw edge down leaving 4cm, gap pleat.

3

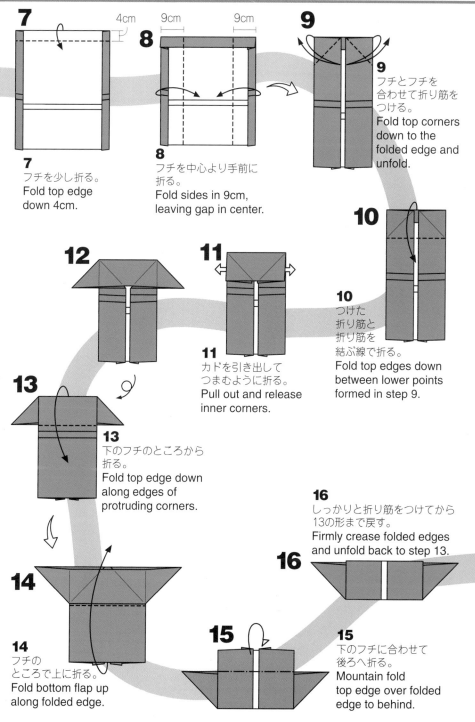

7

4cm

7
フチを少し折る。
Fold top edge
down 4cm.

8

9cm   9cm

8
フチを中心より手前に
折る。
Fold sides in 9cm,
leaving gap in center.

9

9
フチとフチを
合わせて折り筋を
つける。
Fold top corners
down to the
folded edge and
unfold.

10

10
つけた
折り筋と
折り筋を
結ぶ線で折る。
Fold top edges down
between lower points
formed in step 9.

11

11
カドを引き出して
つまむように折る。
Pull out and release
inner corners.

12

13

13
下のフチのところから
折る。
Fold top edge down
along edges of
protruding corners.

14

14
フチの
ところで上に折る。
Fold bottom flap up
along folded edge.

15

15
下のフチに合わせて
後ろへ折る。
Mountain fold
top edge over folded
edge to behind.

16

16
しっかりと折り筋をつけてから
13の形まで戻す。
Firmly crease folded edges
and unfold back to step 13.

Variation

紙／45cm×45cm
仕上がり
／9.5cm×19cm
Paper: 45cm x 45cm
Finished size:
9.5cm x 19cm

正方形の紙で6から同じに折るとカード入れ
のないタイプのさいふができます。
Beginning with your paper in step 6,
complete the folding directions to create
a simple wallet without pockets for cards.

仕上がり／9.5cm×17.4cm
Finished size: 9.5cm x 17.4cm

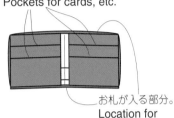

カード類などが
入るポケット。
Pockets for cards, etc.

お札が入る部分。
Location for
paper currency.

22

できあがり
Model complete

21

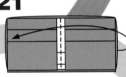

21
半分に折る。
Fold wallet in half
right side to the left.

20

20
フチに合わせて
カドを内側に
折り込む。
Fold side corners
along folded edges
and insert deeply
into pockets.

17

18

19

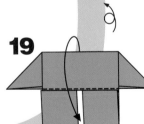

19
13でつけた折り筋で
折る。
Fold top half down
along center crease.

17
14でつけた折り筋で折る。
Fold bottom flap up along
crease made in step 14.

18
15でつけた折り筋でフチを
内側のすきまに折り込む。
Inside-reverse fold top
flap into itself.

フライド ポテト
FRENCH FRIES

カラー口絵Page8

ポテトは紙の長さを変えて折ってみましょう。

Try folding the potato sticks from various lengths of paper for an interesting effect.

紙·Paper Dimension
15cm×15cm···1
7.5cm×7.5cm···6

5
フチのところでカドを
すきまに差し込む。
Insert top upper layer
into pocket in front flap.

6

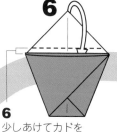

6
少しあけてカドを
内側に折り込む。
Leaving a slight gap,
insert remaining top
point into rear pocket.

5

4
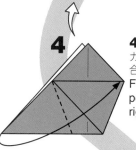

4
カドをフチに
合わせて折る。
Fold lower left
point to touch
right corner.

3
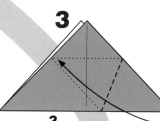

3
カドをフチに合わせて折る。
Fold lower right point to
the left side as shown.

容器／Container

1

1
三角に
折り筋をつける。
White side up, fold in half
diagonally and unfold.

2

2
三角に折る。
Fold bottom point up.

115

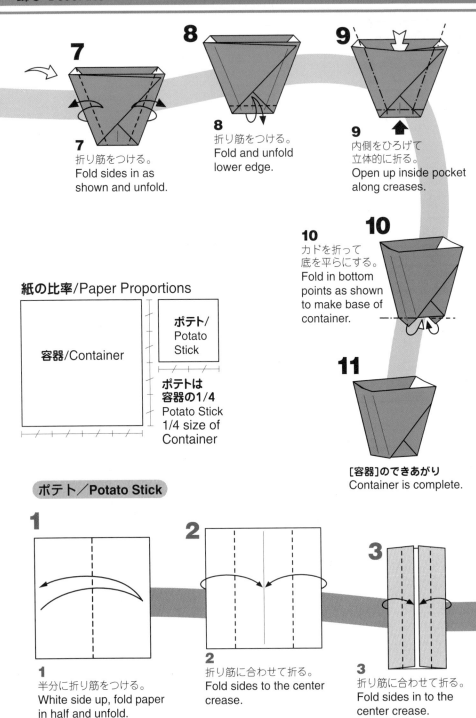

7

7
折り筋をつける。
Fold sides in as
shown and unfold.

8

8
折り筋をつける。
Fold and unfold
lower edge.

9

9
内側をひろげて
立体的に折る。
Open up inside pocket
along creases.

10

10
カドを折って
底を平らにする。
Fold in bottom
points as shown
to make base of
container.

11

[容器]のできあがり
Container is complete.

紙の比率/Paper Proportions

容器/Container

ポテト/
Potato
Stick

ポテトは
容器の1/4
Potato Stick
1/4 size of
Container

ポテト／Potato Stick

1

1
半分に折り筋をつける。
White side up, fold paper
in half and unfold.

2

2
折り筋に合わせて折る。
Fold sides to the center
crease.

3

3
折り筋に合わせて折る。
Fold sides in to the
center crease.

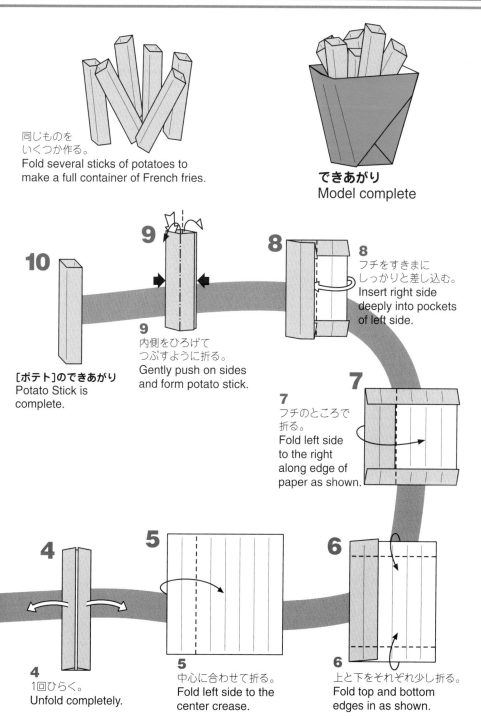

同じものを
いくつか作る。
Fold several sticks of potatoes to
make a full container of French fries.

できあがり
Model complete

10

[ポテト]のできあがり
Potato Stick is
complete.

9

9
内側をひろげて
つぶすように折る。
Gently push on sides
and form potato stick.

8

8
フチをすきまに
しっかりと差し込む。
Insert right side
deeply into pockets
of left side.

7

7
フチのところで
折る。
Fold left side
to the right
along edge of
paper as shown.

4

4
1回ひらく。
Unfold completely.

5

5
中心に合わせて折る。
Fold left side to the
center crease.

6

6
上と下をそれぞれ少し折る。
Fold top and bottom
edges in as shown.

117

ベビーシューズ

BABY SHOES

カラー口絵Page6

かわいい赤ちゃんの靴です。厚手の紙で大きく折ればギフトボックスにもなります。

This is a cute baby bootee. If you fold it from larger, sturdy paper you can make a gift box suitable for favors at baby shower.

紙・Paper Dimension

15cm×15cm・・・2

6

フチに合わせて折る。
Fold left side down to line up with raw edges of right flap.

6

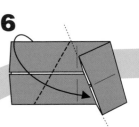

5

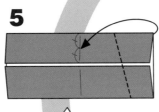

5

カドを折り筋の1/2のところに合わせて折る。
Fold right side to the left bringing top right corner to the mid-point of top flap as shown.

4

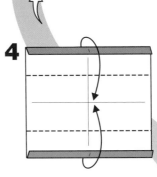

4

折り筋に合わせて折る。
Fold top and bottom edges to the center crease.

1

白い面を上にして半分に折り、広げる。

1

半分に折り筋をつける。
White side up, fold paper in half and unfold.

2

2

フチを少し折る。
Fold top and bottom edges in a little.

3

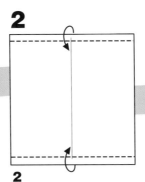

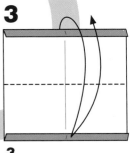

3

フチとフチを合わせて折り筋をつける。
Fold top down to the bottom and unfold.

7

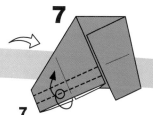

7
巻くように折る。
Fold and roll up
left side as shown.

8

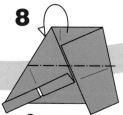

8
半分に後ろへ折る。
Mountain fold top
half behind.

9

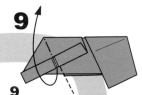

9
フチの中心をつまむように
引き上げる。
Lift and raise left side up.

10

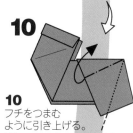

10
フチをつまむ
ように引き上げる。
Lift and raise right side up.

11

11
内側に折る。
Mountain fold bottom edge
in and repeat behind.

12

12
カドを内側に折る。
Mountain fold corners
of toe area in.

13

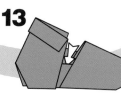

13
矢印のところに指を入れて
内側をひろげて立体的にする。
Open and insert fingers
into pocket to form shoe.

14

14
リボンをすきまに通して結ぶ。
Insert and tie ribbon
under top rim of shoe.

15

同じものを2つ作る。
Make two pieces
like this.

できあがり
Model complete

119

ワイシャツとネクタイ
DRESS SHIRT & NECKTIE

カラー口絵Page7

紙のサイズを変えれば、ギフトラッピングとして父の日などに活用できます。

If you fold these models from larger paper, it will make a suitable giftwrap for a Father's Day gift.

紙・Paper Dimension

ワイシャツ(紙袋)/
22cm×17cm···1
ネクタイ/15cm×15cm···1

6

中心に合わせて折る。
Fold top folded edge down to the center crease.

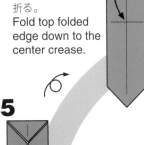

7

カドのところを目安に折る。
Fold flap up at base of triangle.

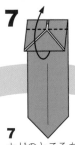

5

4

カドのところから折る。
Fold top corner down.

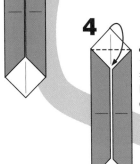

3

中心に合わせて折る。
Fold sides to the center crease.

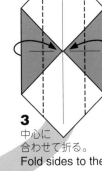

ネクタイ／ Necktie

1

三角に折り筋をつける。
White side up, fold in half diagonally both ways and unfold.

2

カドを中心に折る。
Fold side corners to the center.

120

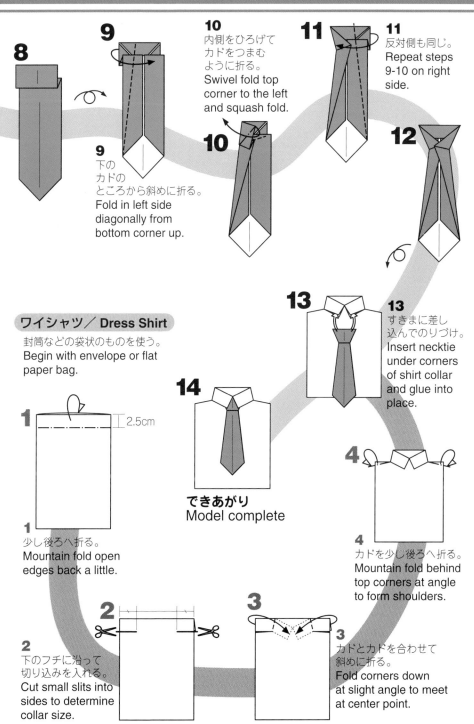

8

9

9
下の
カドの
ところから斜めに折る。
Fold in left side
diagonally from
bottom corner up.

10
内側をひろげて
カドをつまむ
ように折る。
Swivel fold top
corner to the left
and squash fold.

10

11

11
反対側も同じ。
Repeat steps
9-10 on right
side.

12

13

13
すきまに差し
込んでのりづけ。
Insert necktie
under corners
of shirt collar
and glue into
place.

14

できあがり
Model complete

ワイシャツ／ Dress Shirt

封筒などの袋状のものを使う。
Begin with envelope or flat
paper bag.

1
2.5cm

1
少し後ろへ折る。
Mountain fold open
edges back a little.

2
下のフチに沿って
切り込みを入れる。
Cut small slits into
sides to determine
collar size.

3
カドとカドを合わせて
斜めに折る。
Fold corners down
at slight angle to meet
at center point.

4
カドを少し後ろへ折る。
Mountain fold behind
top corners at angle
to form shoulders.

121

ゆびわ
RING

カラー口絵Page7

7.5～8cmの紙で折ると実際に
指にはめるサイズのものができ
ます。

If you use 7.5 - 8 cm
square paper, you can
make a ring you can wear.

紙・Paper Dimension

7.5cm×7.5cm・・・1

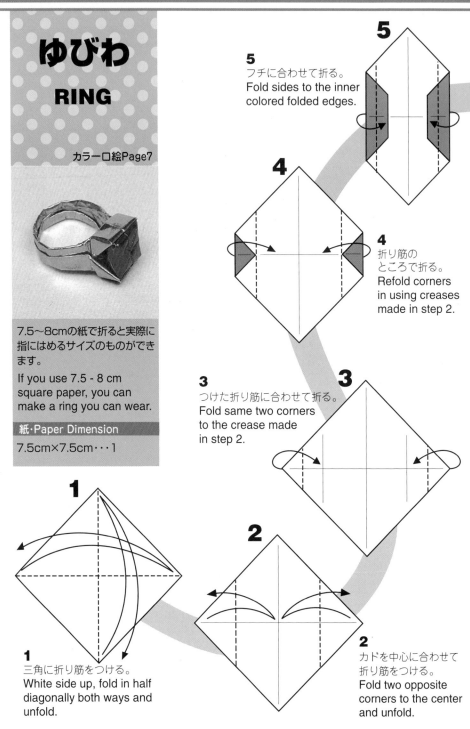

5

フチに合わせて折る。
Fold sides to the inner
colored folded edges.

4

折り筋の
ところで折る。
Refold corners
in using creases
made in step 2.

3

つけた折り筋に合わせて折る。
Fold same two corners
to the crease made
in step 2.

1

三角に折り筋をつける。
White side up, fold in half
diagonally both ways and
unfold.

2

カドを中心に合わせて
折り筋をつける。
Fold two opposite
corners to the center
and unfold.

122

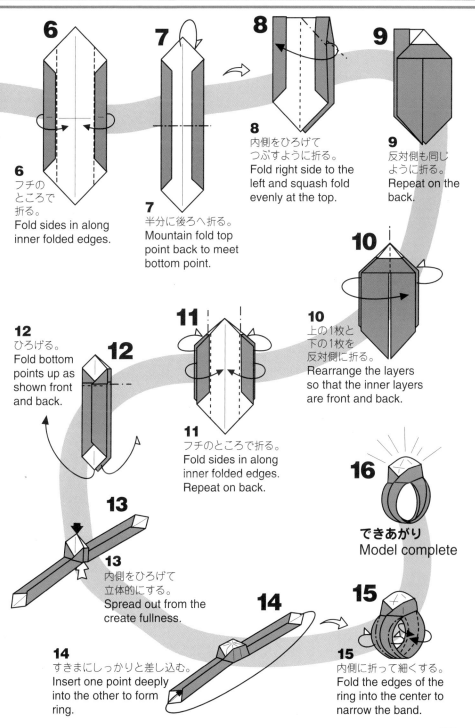

6
フチの
ところで
折る。
Fold sides in along
inner folded edges.

7
半分に後ろへ折る。
Mountain fold top
point back to meet
bottom point.

8
内側をひろげて
つぶすように折る。
Fold right side to the
left and squash fold
evenly at the top.

9
反対側も同じ
ように折る。
Repeat on the
back.

10
上の1枚と
下の1枚を
反対側に折る。
Rearrange the layers
so that the inner layers
are front and back.

11
フチのところで折る。
Fold sides in along
inner folded edges.
Repeat on back.

12
ひろげる。
Fold bottom
points up as
shown front
and back.

13
内側をひろげて
立体的にする。
Spread out from the
create fullness.

14
すきまにしっかりと差し込む。
Insert one point deeply
into the other to form
ring.

15
内側に折って細くする。
Fold the edges of the
ring into the center to
narrow the band.

16
できあがり
Model complete

123

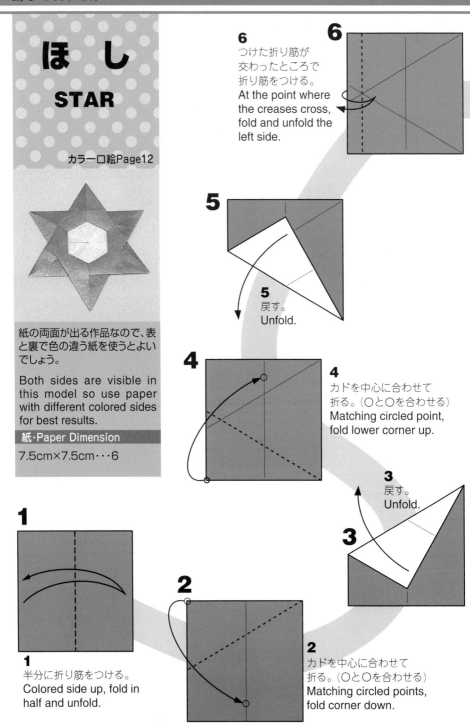

ほし
STAR

カラー口絵Page12

紙の両面が出る作品なので、表と裏で色の違う紙を使うとよいでしょう。

Both sides are visible in this model so use paper with different colored sides for best results.

紙·Paper Dimension

7.5cm×7.5cm···6

6
つけた折り筋が交わったところで折り筋をつける。
At the point where the creases cross, fold and unfold the left side.

5
戻す。
Unfold.

4
カドを中心に合わせて折る。(○と○を合わせる)
Matching circled point, fold lower corner up.

3
戻す。
Unfold.

2
カドを中心に合わせて折る。(○と○を合わせる)
Matching circled points, fold corner down.

1
半分に折り筋をつける。
Colored side up, fold in half and unfold.

124

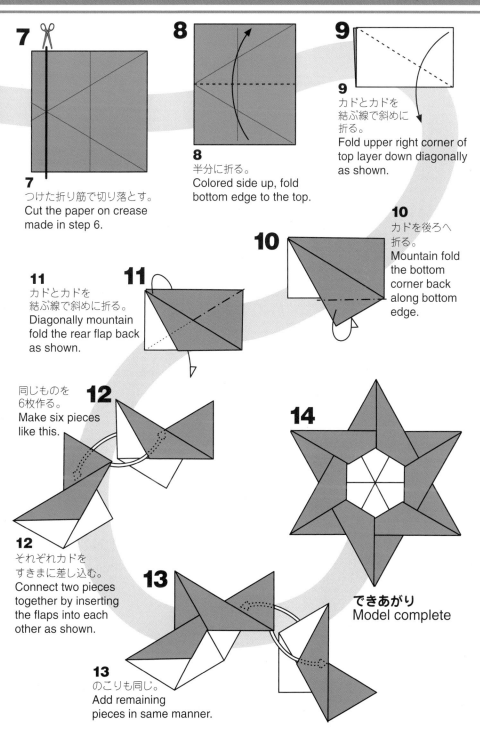

7

つけた折り筋で切り落とす。
Cut the paper on crease
made in step 6.

8
半分に折る。
Colored side up, fold
bottom edge to the top.

9
カドとカドを
結ぶ線で斜めに
折る。
Fold upper right corner of
top layer down diagonally
as shown.

10
カドを後ろへ
折る。
Mountain fold
the bottom
corner back
along bottom
edge.

11
カドとカドを
結ぶ線で斜めに折る。
Diagonally mountain
fold the rear flap back
as shown.

同じものを
6枚作る。
Make six pieces
like this.

12
それぞれカドを
すきまに差し込む。
Connect two pieces
together by inserting
the flaps into each
other as shown.

13
のこりも同じ。
Add remaining
pieces in same manner.

14
できあがり
Model complete

125

スノーマンの
帽子
SNOWMAN'S
HAT

カラー口絵Page13

かんたんに折れる作品です。ス
ノーマンの大きさに合わせて紙
の大きさを調節して下さい。

This is an easy model to
make. Depending upon
the size of the snowman,
adjust the size of your
paper to make the hat.

紙・Paper Dimension

3.5cm×3.5cm···1

7
フチのところで下に折る。
Fold upper layer down
over the bottom white
layer.

7

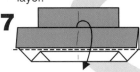

8

8
後ろへ折る。
Mountain fold the
lower edge back to
narrow the brim of hat.

6
つけた折り筋に合わせて
折る。
Fold top edge down and
fold bottom folded edge
up to meet at horizontal
crease.

6

5

5
折り筋をつける。
Fold top layer
down as shown
and unfold.

4

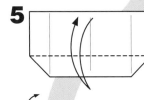

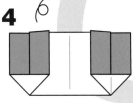

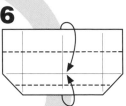

1

3

2
フチを1/3の幅で
それぞれ折る。
Fold both sides in 1/3.

2

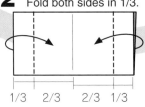

1/3　2/3　2/3　1/3

1
たて半分に折り筋をつけてから
半分に折る。
Colored side up, fold paper
in half both ways.

3
内側をひろげてつぶす
ように折る。
With folded edge at
the bottom, squash
fold the sides flat
evenly.

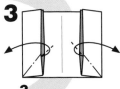

9

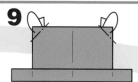

9
1/3ぐらいのところで折る。
Mountain fold back the corners of the hat at about 1/3 point.

10

10
それぞれカドを後ろへ折る。
Mountain fold back smaller corners to round off the hat.

11

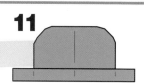

できあがり
Model complete

スノーマンの ミトン

SNOWMAN'S MITTEN

カラー口絵Page12-13

簡単に折れるかわいいミトンです。カードやツリーの飾りに使って下さい。

This is a cute and simple mitten. You can use this to decorate a card or holiday tree.

紙・Paper Dimension

4cm×2cm・・・2

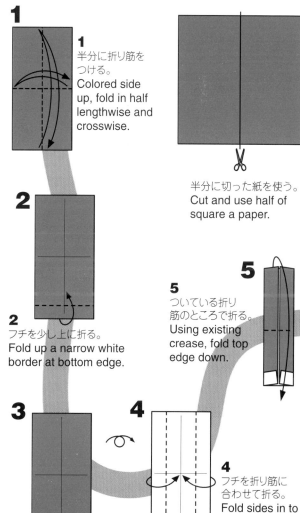

1
半分に折り筋を つける。
Colored side up, fold in half lengthwise and crosswise.

半分に切った紙を使う。
Cut and use half of square a paper.

2
フチを少し上に折る。
Fold up a narrow white border at bottom edge.

3

4
フチを折り筋に合わせて折る。
Fold sides in to meet at center.

5
ついている折り 筋のところで折る。
Using existing crease, fold top edge down.

127

スノーマン
SNOWMAN

カラー口絵Page12-13

白が出るように紙の裏を使って
下さい。かおをかき込んでもか
わいいですね。

Use the backside of origami
paper so white side will show.
Draw in a face for nice results.

紙・Paper Dimension

5.5cm×5.5cm‥‥1

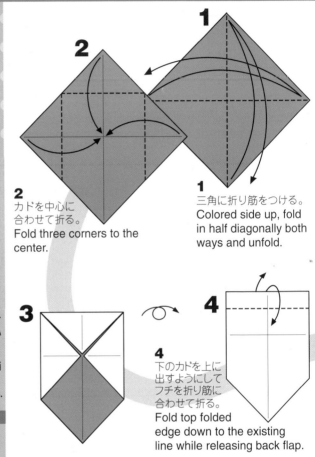

2
カドを中心に
合わせて折る。
Fold three corners to the
center.

1
三角に折り筋をつける。
Colored side up, fold
in half diagonally both
ways and unfold.

4
下のカドを上に
出すようにして
フチを折り筋に
合わせて折る。
Fold top folded
edge down to the existing
line while releasing back flap.

6
斜めに上に折る。
Fold top layer
diagonally to the
right as shown.

7
引き寄せるように折る。
Swivel fold left side
of top layer as shown.

左側は6から左右反対に折る。
To make the left side of the
pair, reverse the directions
from step 6.

8
それぞれカドを少し折る。
Fold small triangles to
round the corners.

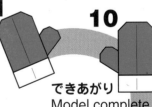

できあがり
Model complete

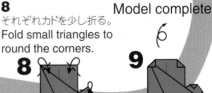

128

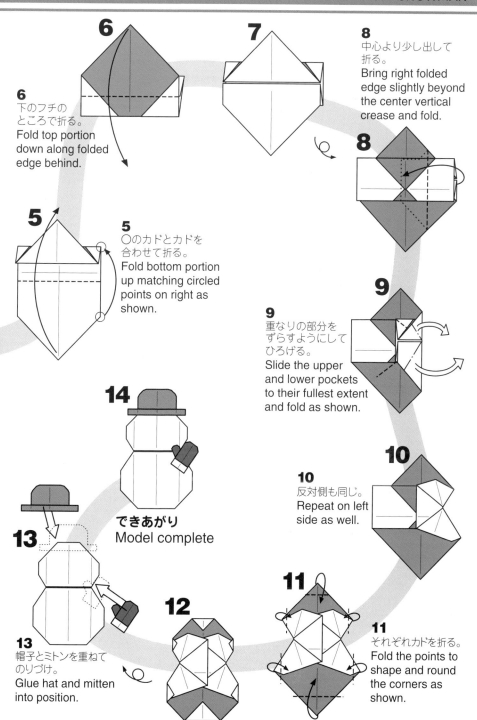

6

6
下のフチの
ところで折る。
Fold top portion
down along folded
edge behind.

7

8
中心より少し出して
折る。
Bring right folded
edge slightly beyond
the center vertical
crease and fold.

8

5

5
○のカドとカドを
合わせて折る。
Fold bottom portion
up matching circled
points on right as
shown.

9
重なりの部分を
ずらすようにして
ひろげる。
Slide the upper
and lower pockets
to their fullest extent
and fold as shown.

9

10

10
反対側も同じ。
Repeat on left
side as well.

14

できあがり
Model complete

13

13
帽子とミトンを重ねて
のりづけ。
Glue hat and mitten
into position.

12

11

11
それぞれカドを折る。
Fold the points to
shape and round
the corners as
shown.

129

キャンドル

CANDLE

カラー口絵Page12-13

1枚でろうそくと炎を表現した作品です。表と裏で色の違う紙を使いましょう。

The candle and flame are folded out of a single sheet of paper. Therefore, use paper with two different colored sides for best results.

紙・Paper Dimension

6cm×3cm・・・1

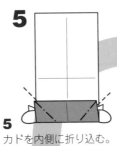

5

カドを内側に折り込む。
Inside-reverse fold corners.

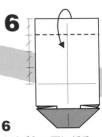

6

1/4ぐらい下に折る。
Fold top edge down about 1/4 as shown.

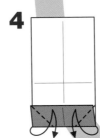

4

三角に折り筋をつける。
Fold corners and unfold.

3

1/3ぐらい上に折る。
Fold up lower edge about 1/3 as shown.

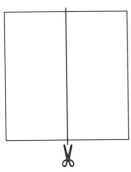

半分に切った紙を使う。
Cut and use half of square a paper.

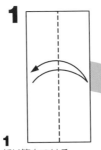

1

折り筋をつける。
White side up, fold in half lengthwise and unfold.

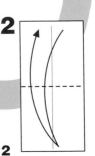

2

半分に折り筋をつける。
Fold in half cross-wise.

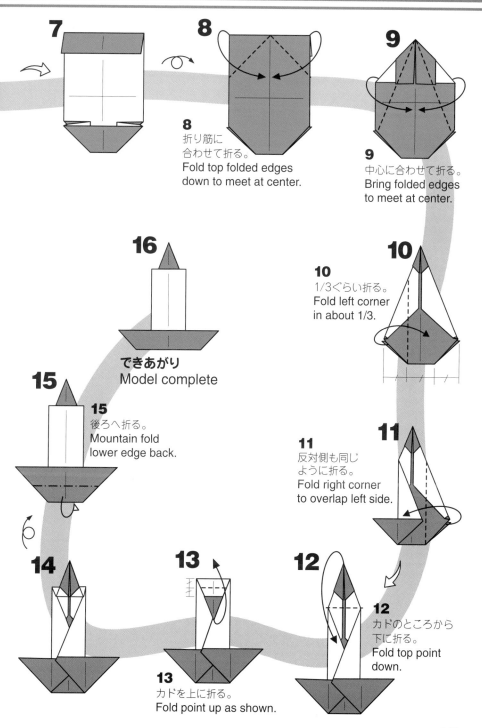

7

8

折り筋に
合わせて折る。
Fold top folded edges
down to meet at center.

9

中心に合わせて折る。
Bring folded edges
to meet at center.

16

10

1/3ぐらい折る。
Fold left corner
in about 1/3.

10

できあがり
Model complete

15

後ろへ折る。
Mountain fold
lower edge back.

11

反対側も同じ
ように折る。
Fold right corner
to overlap left side.

11

14

13

カドを上に折る。
Fold point up as shown.

12

12

カドのところから
下に折る。
Fold top point
down.

くつした

SOCK

カラー口絵Page12-13

折る紙の色や柄を変えてバリエーションを作ってみましょう。カードと大きさを合わせて下さい。

You can experiment using various colors and prints for different results. If using on the card, adjust the size of the paper to fit.

紙・Paper Dimension

6cm×6cm···1

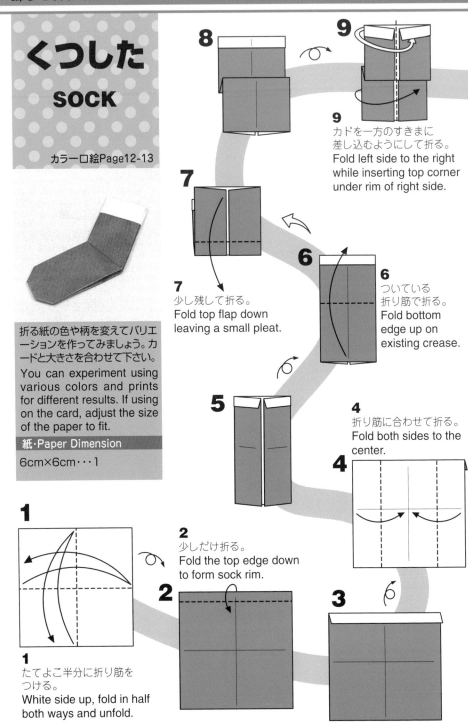

8

9

9
カドを一方のすきまに差し込むようにして折る。
Fold left side to the right while inserting top corner under rim of right side.

7

7
少し残して折る。
Fold top flap down leaving a small pleat.

6

6
ついている折り筋で折る。
Fold bottom edge up on existing crease.

5

4

4
折り筋に合わせて折る。
Fold both sides to the center.

1

2
少しだけ折る。
Fold the top edge down to form sock rim.

2

3

1
たてよこ半分に折り筋をつける。
White side up, fold in half both ways and unfold.

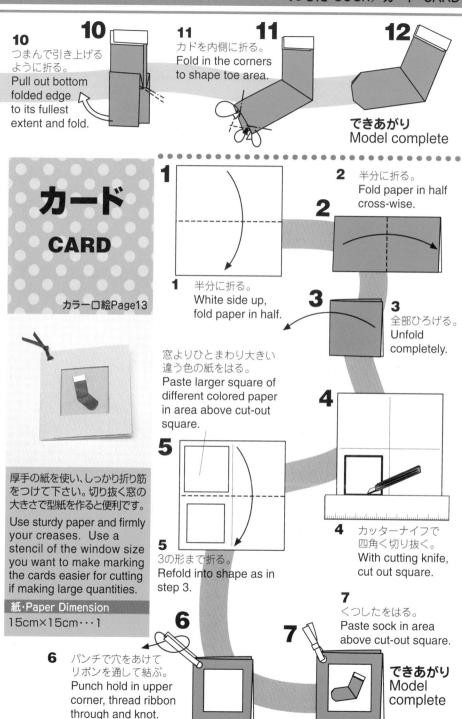

10
つまんで引き上げる
ように折る。
Pull out bottom
folded edge
to its fullest
extent and fold.

11
カドを内側に折る。
Fold in the corners
to shape toe area.

12
できあがり
Model complete

カード
CARD
カラー口絵Page13

厚手の紙を使い、しっかり折り筋
をつけて下さい。切り抜く窓の
大きさで型紙を作ると便利です。

Use sturdy paper and firmly
your creases. Use a
stencil of the window size
you want to make marking
the cards easier for cutting
if making large quantities.

紙・Paper Dimension
15cm×15cm・・・1

1
半分に折る。
White side up,
fold paper in half.

2
半分に折る。
Fold paper in half
cross-wise.

3
全部ひろげる。
Unfold
completely.

4
カッターナイフで
四角く切り抜く。
With cutting knife,
cut out square.

窓よりひとまわり大きい
違う色の紙をはる。
Paste larger square of
different colored paper
in area above cut-out
square.

5
3の形まで折る。
Refold into shape as in
step 3.

6
パンチで穴をあけて
リボンを通して結ぶ。
Punch hold in upper
corner, thread ribbon
through and knot.

7
くつしたをはる。
Paste sock in area
above cut-out square.

できあがり
Model
complete

ブーツ
BOOTS

カラー口絵Page12

立体にするときに形が均等になるように注意して下さい。

When forming the final shape, take care to open the model up evenly.

紙・Paper Dimension

6cm×6cm···2

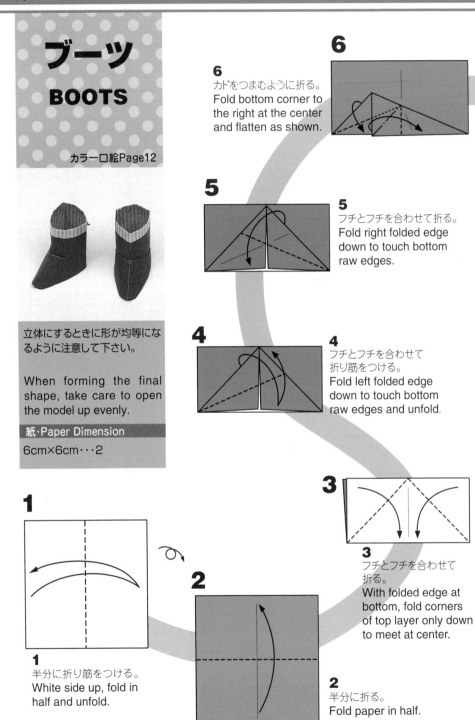

6
カドをつまむように折る。
Fold bottom corner to the right at the center and flatten as shown.

5
フチとフチを合わせて折る。
Fold right folded edge down to touch bottom raw edges.

4
フチとフチを合わせて折り筋をつける。
Fold left folded edge down to touch bottom raw edges and unfold.

3
フチとフチを合わせて折る。
With folded edge at bottom, fold corners of top layer only down to meet at center.

1
半分に折り筋をつける。
White side up, fold in half and unfold.

2
半分に折る。
Fold paper in half.

7

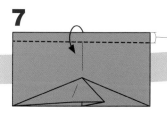

7
こちら側の幅を
少しひろく
フチを下に折る。
Fold top edge
down making
right side slightly
wider than left.

8

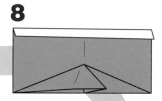

9

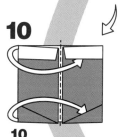

9
中心に合わせて折る。
Fold both sides in to
meet at center crease.

10

10
カドをすきまに折り込む。
Fold left side to the right
while inserting corners
into pockets as shown.

左側は7から左右反対に折る。
To make the left side of
the pair, reverse the
directions from step 7.

13

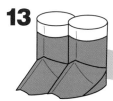

できあがり
Model complete

12
内側をひろげて立体的にして
形を整える。
Open the top folded edges
and shape with fingers to
form boot.

12

11

11
カドを内側に折る。
Inside-reverse fold
toe point of boot.

サンタ クロース
SANTA CLAUS

カラー口絵Page12

少し折りが細かいですが、てい
ねいに折って下さい。

The folds in this model are
small so make your
creases carefully.

紙・Paper Dimension
12cm×12cm···1
3cm×3cm···1

1 からだ／ Body

1
半分に折る。
White side up, fold paper
in half.

2
半分に折る。
Fold right side to
the left side.

3
内側をひろげて
つぶすように折る。
Open top layer and
squash fold corner
to the right.

4

5
反対側に折る。
Fold flap on right all
the way to the left.

6
内側をひろげて
つぶすように折る。
Open top layer and
squash fold corner
to the right.

7
カドとカドを合わせて折る。
Fold corners of top
layers to the top
point.

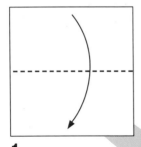

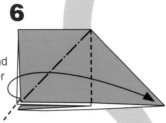
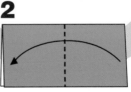

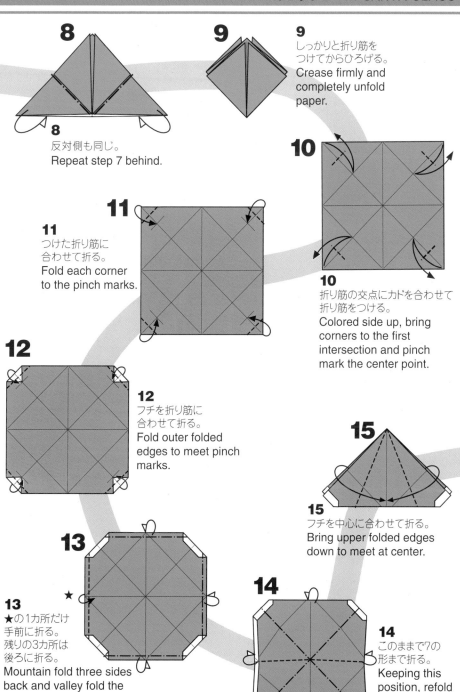

8

8
反対側も同じ。
Repeat step 7 behind.

9

9
しっかりと折り筋を
つけてからひろげる。
Crease firmly and
completely unfold
paper.

10

10
折り筋の交点にカドを合わせて
折り筋をつける。
Colored side up, bring
corners to the first
intersection and pinch
mark the center point.

11

11
つけた折り筋に
合わせて折る。
Fold each corner
to the pinch marks.

12

12
フチを折り筋に
合わせて折る。
Fold outer folded
edges to meet pinch
marks.

15

15
フチを中心に合わせて折る。
Bring upper folded edges
down to meet at center.

13

13
★の1カ所だけ
手前に折る。
残りの3カ所は
後ろに折る。
Mountain fold three sides
back and valley fold the
remaining side to make a
narrow white border.

14

14
このままで7の
形まで折る。
Keeping this
position, refold
into step 7.

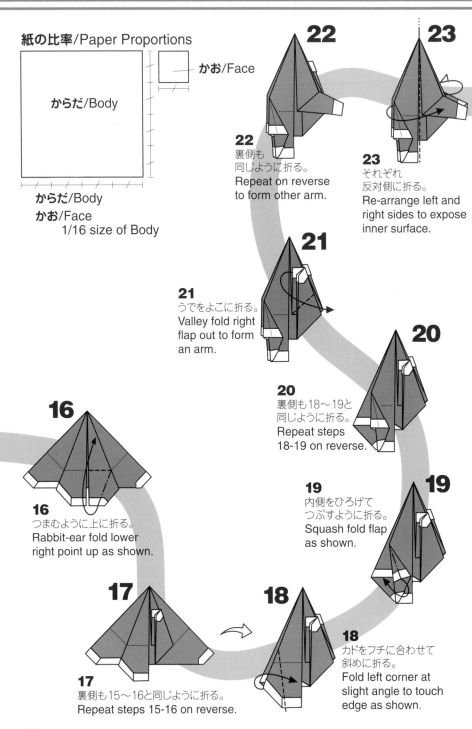

紙の比率/Paper Proportions

かお/Face

からだ/Body

からだ/Body
かお/Face
1/16 size of Body

22

22
裏側も
同じように折る。
Repeat on reverse
to form other arm.

23

23
それぞれ
反対側に折る。
Re-arrange left and
right sides to expose
inner surface.

21

21
うでをよこに折る。
Valley fold right
flap out to form
an arm.

20

20
裏側も18〜19と
同じように折る。
Repeat steps
18-19 on reverse.

19

19
内側をひろげて
つぶすように折る。
Squash fold flap
as shown.

16

16
つまむように上に折る。
Rabbit-ear fold lower
right point up as shown.

17

17
裏側も15〜16と同じように折る。
Repeat steps 15-16 on reverse.

18

18
カドをフチに合わせて
斜めに折る。
Fold left corner at
slight angle to touch
edge as shown.

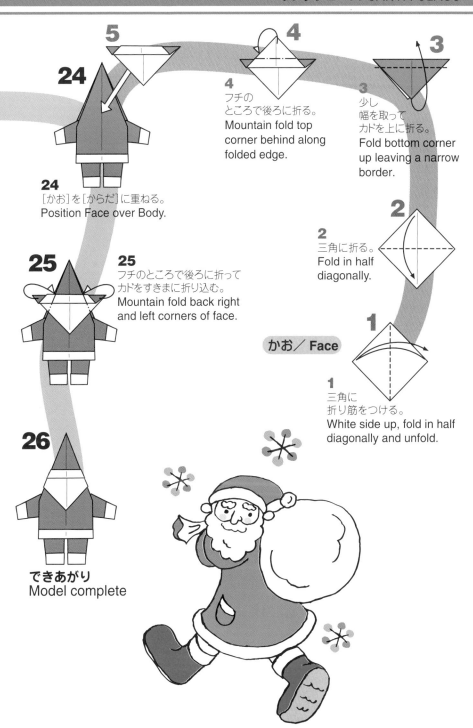

5

24

4

フチの
ところで後ろに折る。
Mountain fold top
corner behind along
folded edge.

3

少し
幅を取って
カドを上に折る。
Fold bottom corner
up leaving a narrow
border.

24
[かお]を[からだ]に重ねる。
Position Face over Body.

2

三角に折る。
Fold in half
diagonally.

25

25
フチのところで後ろに折って
カドをすきまに折り込む。
Mountain fold back right
and left corners of face.

1

かお／**Face**

1
三角に
折り筋をつける。
White side up, fold in half
diagonally and unfold.

26

できあがり
Model complete

クリスマス ツリー

STACKING CHRISTMAS TREE

カラー口絵Page12

しっかりした厚手の紙を使うと良いでしょう。他の作品を小さく折って飾って下さい。

Using stiff paper, you can make an attractive tree. It can support small pieces of origami and other decorations to make a pretty display.

紙・Paper Dimension
11cm×11cm,13.5cm×13.5cm,15cm×15cm,17.5cm×17.5cm
各1枚／1 sheet each
20cm×20cm, 2枚／2 sheets

6
内側をひろげて
つぶすように折る。
Open top layer to the left and squash fold bottom right corner up.

5
カドを反対側に折る。
Fold left flap all the way to the right.

3
内側をひろげて
つぶすように折る。
Open top layer to the left and squash fold bottom right corner up.

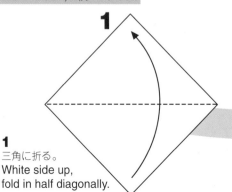

1
三角に折る。
White side up,
fold in half diagonally.

2
三角に折る。
Fold left corner to the right.

葉／Branches

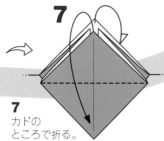

7

7
カドの
ところで折る。
Fold top corner down to the
bottom and repeat behind.

8

8
戻す。
Unfold.

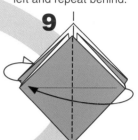

9
それぞれ反対側に折る。
Fold top right flap to the
left and repeat behind.

9

10

10
カドのところで
折り筋をつける。
Fold top corner
down to the bottom
and unfold. Repeat
behind.

11

11
カドとカドを
合わせて折る。
Fold top corner down
to the left corner.

幹／Trunk

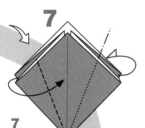

7

7
中心に
合わせて折る
反対側も同じ。
Fold left folded edge
to the center crease
and repeat behind.

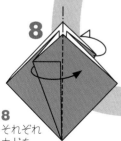

8

8
それぞれ
カドを
反対側に折る。
Fold left flap to
the right and
repeat behind.

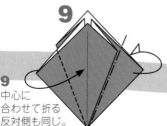

9

9
中心に
合わせて折る
反対側も同じ。
Fold left folded edge to
the center crease and
repeat behind.

10

10
フチのところで
折り筋をつける。
Fold top corner
down along folded
edge of flap and unfold.

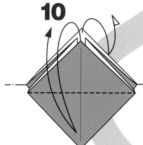

141

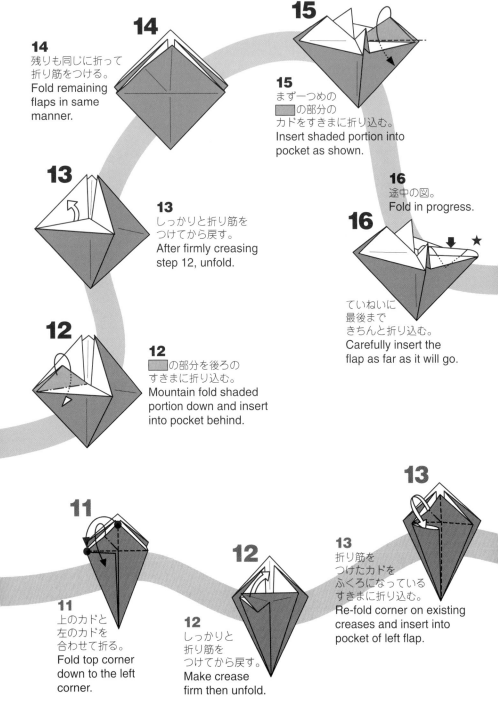

14
残りも同じに折って
折り筋をつける。
Fold remaining
flaps in same
manner.

15
まず一つめの
▢の部分の
カドをすきまに折り込む。
Insert shaded portion into
pocket as shown.

16
途中の図。
Fold in progress.

13
しっかりと折り筋を
つけてから戻す。
After firmly creasing
step 12, unfold.

ていねいに
最後まで
きちんと折り込む。
Carefully insert the
flap as far as it will go.

12
▢の部分を後ろの
すきまに折り込む。
Mountain fold shaded
portion down and insert
into pocket behind.

11
上のカドと
左のカドを
合わせて折る。
Fold top corner
down to the left
corner.

12
しっかりと
折り筋を
つけてから戻す。
Make crease
firm then unfold.

13
折り筋を
つけたカドを
ふくろになっている
すきまに折り込む。
Re-fold corner on existing
creases and insert into
pocket of left flap.

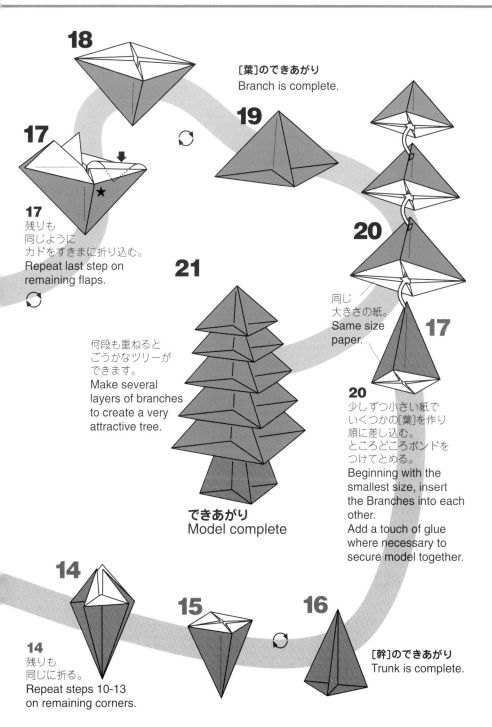

18

[葉]のできあがり
Branch is complete.

19

17

17
残りも
同じように
カドをすきまに折り込む。
Repeat last step on
remaining flaps.

20

21

同じ
大きさの紙。
Same size
paper.

17

何段も重ねると
ごうかなツリーが
できます。
Make several
layers of branches
to create a very
attractive tree.

20
少しずつ小さい紙で
いくつかの[葉]を作り
順に差し込む。
ところどころボンドを
つけてとめる。
Beginning with the
smallest size, insert
the Branches into each
other.
Add a touch of glue
where necessary to
secure model together.

できあがり
Model complete

14

15

16

14
残りも
同じに折る。
Repeat steps 10-13
on remaining corners.

[幹]のできあがり
Trunk is complete.

143

山口真（やまぐち まこと）
1944年、東京生まれ。日本折紙協会事務局員を経て折り紙作家として活躍。
1989年、折り紙専門の常設ギャラリー「おりがみはうす」を開設。ここを拠
点に若手作家の育成、海外の折り紙団体や作家との精力的な交流を行っている。
日本折紙学会評議員兼事務局長。日本折紙協会理事。OrigamiUSA会員。
British Origami Society会員。雑誌『折紙探偵団』編集長。主な著書に、『暮ら
しに役立つ実用折り紙』『おりがみ辞典』(西東社)、『たのしい折り紙ワールド』
『たのしい折り紙全集』『すてきな折り紙』(主婦と生活社)、『日本のおりがみ
事典』『たのしいおりがみ事典』(ナツメ社)、『トーヨーのおりがみブックシリ
ーズ』(トーヨー) など多数。

ギャラリーおりがみはうす
〒113-0001　東京都文京区白山1-33-8-216
☎(03)5684-6040
日本で最初のおりがみ専門の展示場です。常時折り紙作品の展示を行っています。
（午前10時より午後6時まで。日曜・祭日は休み。入場無料）地下鉄・都営三田線白山駅下車　A1出口前
E-mail:origamih@remus.dti.ne.jp（おりがみはうす）
URL:http://www.remus.dti.ne.jp/~origamih/（おりがみはうす）
URL:http://www.origami.gr.jp/（日本折紙学会）

Yamaguchi Makoto
Born in Tokyo in 1944. Mr. Yamaguchi has taken an active part in origami as a professional creator after working with the
Nippon Origami Association. In1989, he opened "Gallery Origami House", a venue to showcase the works of origami creators.
He has worked hard to encourage young creators to continue to improve their models, to interchange with foreign groups and
creators abroad. His enthusiasm for origami has lead him to become involved with origami associations around the world:
JOAS (Japan Origami Academic Society) Board of Directors President; Board member of NOA (Nippon Origami Association);
member of OrigamiUSA, member of British Origami Society, Chief Editor of "Origami Tanteidan" magazine. His principal books
are: "Kurashi ni Yakudatsu Jitsuyou Origami"; "Origami Jiten" (Seitousha Publishers); "Tanoshii Origami World"; "Tanoshii
Origami Zenshuu"; "Suteki na Origami" (Shufu-to-Seikatsusha Publishers); "Nihon no Origami Jiten" (Natsumesha Publishers);
"Toyo no Origami Book Series" (Toyo Publishers) etc. The list goes on and on.

Gallery Origami House
This is the first place in Japan to specialize in featuring origami as its one and only focus.
There are wonderful origami works of art on display at all times. Admission is free.
It is open daily from 10 a.m. to 6 p.m. Monday through Saturday.
It is closed on Sundays and national holidays.
It is conveniently located across the street from the Toei Mita Line Hakusan Subway Station, A1 exit.
TEL:03-5684-6040●ADDRESS:33-8-216 Hakusan 1-chome,Bunkyo-ku,Tokyo 〒113-0001

折り図・折り紙製作／おりがみはうす（山口真・田尻敦士・松浦英子）
英訳／June Sakamoto
口絵レイアウト／太田由美子（レフア）
撮影／梅野寛康（上牧写真事務所）
イラスト／伊藤弘美

編集協力／株式会社童夢

英語訳つき おりがみ
Let's Enjoy Origami in English and Japanese

●協定により検印省略

著　者　山口　真
発行者　池田　豊
印刷所　図書印刷株式会社
製本所　図書印刷株式会社
発行所　株式会社池田書店
　　　　東京都新宿区弁天町43番地（〒162-0851）
　　　　電話(03)3267-6821(代)／振替00120-9-60072
　　　　落丁・乱丁はおとりかえいたします。

0100007